RENT REVIEW

RENT REVIEW

John Male QC

and

Thomas Jefferies

Landmark Chambers

ACKNOWLEDGEMENTS

The authors and publishers wish to thank the following for permission to reproduce copyright material:

Crown copyright material is reproduced with the permission of the Controller of HMSO and the Queen's Printer for Scotland.

Please note: References to the masculine include, where appropriate, the feminine.

Published by RICS Business Services Limited,
a wholly owned subsidiary of
The Royal Institution of Chartered Surveyors
under the RICS Books imprint
Surveyor Court
Westwood Business Park
Coventry CV4 8JE
UK
www.ricsbooks.com

ISBN 1 84219 225 6

Typeset in Great Britain by Columns Design Ltd, Reading
Printed in Great Britain by Bell & Bain, Glasgow

Contents

Preface

While chartered surveyors may not need the *breadth* of understanding of the law of their opposite numbers in the legal profession, in a number of key areas of application to property and construction they need a similar *depth* of legal knowledge. Exactly what the key areas may be depends to some extent on the nature of the surveyor's practice; two obvious examples are the law of landlord and tenant, and town and country planning. Plenty of chartered surveyors will have more frequent reference to the law in these areas than the average lawyer in a general practice; in fact, they need to know the law as much as the valuation principles in subjects like compulsory purchase compensation, not least because the former can affect the latter.

So surveyors require legal knowledge and for a variety of reasons need to develop their understanding of it. Changing trends or individual variations in clients' requirements mean that from time to time even the best practitioners (perhaps especially the best practitioners) will feel the need to expand their knowledge. The knowledge acquired at college or in studying for the Assessment of Professional Competence has a limited shelf life and needs to be constantly updated to maintain its currency. Even specialists working in their areas of expertise need a source of reference as an aide-memoire or as a first port of call in more detailed research.

The Case in Point series

RICS Books is committed to meeting the needs of surveying (and other) professionals and the Case in Point series typifies that commitment. It is aimed at those who need to upgrade or update their legal knowledge, or who need to have access to a good first reference at the outset of an inquiry. A particular difficulty in doing so lies in the area of case law. There are few legal subjects of interest to surveyors where it does not play a major role. This is true of areas like professional negligence, largely ungoverned by statute, where the cases represent the law. However, it is also true of areas like landlord and tenant – where a statutory framework exists, but where interpretation and application of the provisions at the sharp end are provided by judicial decisions. Chartered surveyors are generally well aware of the importance of case law but are confronted by a significant practical problem in dealing with it, namely, the burgeoning of reported decisions of the courts. The sheer scale of the law reports, both general and specialist, makes it very hard even to be aware of recent trends, let alone identify the significance of a particular decision. Thus it was decided to focus on the developments in case law. In any given matter, the practitioner will want to be directed efficiently and painlessly to the decision which bears upon the matter he or she is dealing with; in other words to 'the case in point'.

The series offers a wealth of legal information, which is essential in its application to the surveyor's work. The author of each title has the degree of expertise required to be selective and succinct: thus achieving a high level of relevancy without sacrificing accessibility.

The series is developing incrementally and already comprises a range of specialist handbooks, which can deliver what busy practitioners want – the law on the matter they are handling, when they want it.

Rent Review, John Male QC and Thomas Jefferies

The process of rent review in commercial leases, whereby mechanisms for increases (in practice) in rent form part of the agreement, is one of the most controversial and challenging areas of surveyors' practice and of the law of landlord and tenant. It is a battle-ground between the owners and tenants of a whole range of types of property: offices, shops, warehouses, factories, hotels, restaurants and leisure facilities. It is a battle-ground, moreover, in which government has felt obliged to become engaged: the May 2004 consultation paper from the Office of the Deputy Prime Minister, *Commercial property leases: options for deterring or outlawing the use of upward only rent review clauses*, ignited, or more accurately fuelled, a keen debate between long-entrenched interests; at times an emotive one.

If it is a battle-ground, the ammunition of the parties in the rent review battle is the law. This is true at the 'front-end' of the process, when provisions and dispute resolution procedures are being hammered out in negotiation and drafted, and even more so in the dispute stages, whether the procedure be arbitration, expert determination or challenge in the courts. The greater part of this is modern case law, decided within the last 30–40 years, case law moreover of considerable complexity, encompassing both decisions on particularly arcane facts and statements of general principle.

To take the mass of modern rent review case law and to order it in a way that is practical without being over-simplistic is a task that few lawyers would attempt and fewer still could accomplish. RICS Books has been fortunate to engage members of one of the true heavyweight property law Chambers who have that capability. Landmark Chambers was a 2002 amalgamation of two well-known sets and has over 60 members. John Male QC is one of the leading silks at the property bar and has a substantial rent review practice. Tom Jefferies, a Committee Member of the Property Bar Association, brings nearly 25 years of experience to the subject. Together, they have produced a source of reference that offers many answers and much enlightenment.

Anthony Lavers, 2005.
Professional Support Lawyer, White & Case, London.
Visiting Professor of Law, Oxford Brookes University, Oxford.
Consultant Editor, Case in Point Series.

List of Acts and Statutory Instruments

Access to Justice Act 1999 ('1999 Act')

Arbitration Act 1950 ('1950 Act')
Arbitration Act 1979
Arbitration Act 1996 ('1996 Act')

Civil Evidence Act 1995
Civil Procedure Rules 1998, SI 1998, No. 3132

Landlord and Tenant Act 1927 ('LTA 1927')
Landlord and Tenant Act 1954 ('LTA 1954')

Law of Property Act 1969

Town and Country Planning (Use Classes) Order 1972, SI 1972, No. 1385
Town and Country Planning (Use Classes) Order 1987, SI 1987, No. 764

The text of this publication is divided into commentary and case summaries. The commentary is enclosed between grey highlighted lines for ease of reference.

Table of Cases

1
Introduction

1.1 THE PURPOSE OF A RENT REVIEW CLAUSE

Rent review clauses are a feature of almost every modern commercial lease which is granted for a term of any significant length. The general purpose of such a clause has been described by the courts as to enable the landlord to obtain from time to time the market rental which the premises would command if let on the same terms in the open market at the review dates. The purpose is to reflect the changes in the value of money and real increases in the value of the property during a long term. It has also been said by the courts that the general object of a rent review clause is to provide the landlord with some means of relief where, through increases in property values or falls in the value of money, in an inflationary period, a fixed rent has become out of date and unduly favourable to the tenant. The exact measure of relief depends on the true construction of the review clause.

A court will normally have regard to these statements of the general purpose or object of a rent review clause when construing the clause. It is, however, unrealistic to regard rent review clauses as not at all for the benefit of the tenant. Without such a clause the tenant would never get the length of lease and the security which he requires and to that extent the clause is for the benefit of the tenant.

British Gas Corporation v Universities Superannuation Scheme Ltd (1986)

The Court had to consider whether the hypothetical lease upon rent review would itself contain rent review clauses. The Court stressed the need to have regard to the underlying commercial purpose of a rent review clause in construing it. Accordingly, in the absence of clear contrary words, future reviews should be assumed in the hypothetical lease in fixing the open market rent under the hypothetical letting.

Basingstoke and Deane Borough Council v Host Group Ltd (1987)

The Court of Appeal stressed the need, when construing a rent review clause, to have in mind what is normally the commercial purpose of such a clause. That purpose is to enable the landlord to obtain from time to time the market rental which the premises would command if let on the same terms on the open market at the review dates and to reflect the changes in the value of money and real increases in the value of property during a long term. In this particular case that purpose was held to apply equally to a long lease at a ground rent as to a shorter lease at a rack rent.

United Scientific Holdings Ltd v Burnley Borough Council (1977)

In considering whether time limits were of the essence of a rent review clause the House of Lords rejected the suggestion that such clauses were options entirely for the benefit of the landlord. The House of Lords stressed that a rent review clause is an inseverable part of the whole consideration of the landlord's grant of a term of years of the length agreed. Without it, in a period during which inflation was anticipated, the landlord would either have been unwilling to grant a lease for a longer period than up to the first review date or would have demanded a higher rent to be paid throughout the term than that payable before the first review date. By the time of each review of rent the tenant will have already received a substantial part of the whole benefit which it was intended that he should obtain in return for his acceptance of the obligation to pay the higher rent for the succeeding period.

1.2 THE LAW RELATING TO RENT REVIEW CLAUSES

It is only over the last 30 or so years that the law relating to rent review clauses has come into existence. There are three main sources of law to be considered. They are:

- case law,
- Acts of Parliament, and
- procedural codes for any application to court.

The greater part of the law relating to rent reviews is contained in case law which has grown up since the 1970s. As and when cases have been decided on particular subjects those who have drafted leases have tried to deal with such decisions by what may seem to some readers to be even more complicated drafting. The principal Act of Parliament which affects rent reviews is the *Arbitration Act* 1996 (the '1996 Act') which normally governs the procedure for rent review arbitrations. The procedural code for any application to court (e.g. appeals under the 1996 Act or claims to set aside an expert's determination or claims for negligence against an expert) is the *Civil Procedure Rules* 1998.

1.3 DIFFERENT KINDS OF RENT REVIEW CLAUSES

Over the years different kinds of rent review clauses have been used in leases. Set out below are some examples of the different kinds.

1.3.1 Fixed increases

The parties sometimes agree a series of identified stepped rents which provides a very basic and simple form of rent review. For example, in a term of ten years the parties may agree to an initial rent of £10,000 per annum increasing by £500 per annum every year and so rising to £14,500 in the last year.

Horford Investments Ltd v Lambert (1974)

Whilst this was a housing case, it concerned a 20-year lease in which the annual rents for three successive periods were £1,298, £1,550 and £1,930.

1.3.2 Turnover rents

The parties may agree that the rent be linked to the turnover of the tenant's business carried on at the premises, subject to a base below which the rent may not fall. If the business prospers the rent will increase and the landlord will benefit from that prosperity. If the business does not prosper the landlord will still receive the base rent. Sometimes, there may be a combination of a fixed, or indexed, rent together with an element of turnover rent.

Tucker v Granada Motorway Services Ltd (1979)

A lease for 50 years of a motorway service area reserved a fixed annual rent of £15,000 and a sum equal to a percentage of gross takings on a sliding scale.

1.3.3 Indexation

The parties may agree that the rent be linked to an index which records changes in the value of money, such as the RPI. Care needs to be taken in the choice of index. Provision needs to be made in the clause for matters such as the rebasing or the abolition of the index.

Blumenthal v Gallery Five Ltd (1971)

This rent review clause provided for reviews based on the Index of Retail Prices. The expression 'retail prices' was held to include anything which could be said to have a retail price which included matters such as rents, rates and transport fares.

Wyndham Investments Ltd v Motorway Tyres and Accessories Ltd (1991)

A rent review clause provided for reviews by reference to indexation. The Court of Appeal could not make the indexation clause operate sensibly with the result that a fallback provision in the clause had to be invoked.

1.3.4 Ground rent reviews

In some cases, such as where the landlord provides only the land and the tenant constructs the building, the parties may agree a ground rent subject to review.

Guildford Borough Council v Cobb (1994)

A lease of land on which the tenant had erected industrial buildings provided for a review to be 'the then current ground rental value of the demised premises'. It was held that the rent to be determined should be a ground rent.

Braid v Walsall Metropolitan Borough Council (1998)

A lease for 60 years was granted of a piece of vacant undeveloped land with a covenant by the tenant to erect buildings on the land. The rent review clause required a review to 'a reasonable rent for the land'. It was held that the reference to 'the land' in the review clause required a review disregarding the buildings at any time standing on the land.

1.3.5 Geared rent reviews

In some cases the parties may agree that the rent shall be a particular proportion of the open market rental value or a share of subrents received or receivable by the tenant.

British Railways Board v Elgar House Ltd (1969)

In a lease for 120 years the landlord was to receive an 'equity rent equal to one third of any rack rents received by the tenant in respect of sublettings of the demised premises in excess of £22,000'. It was held that this applied to any part of the building occupied by the tenant and that the language used was capable of extending to the rents which could be obtained for parts which were unlet.

Ashworth Frazer Ltd v Gloucester City Council (1995)

In a building lease for 114 years the rent was to be 8% of 'the rack rents receivable'. It was held that these words were to be given a wide construction of the 'rack rents capable of being received'.

1.3.6 Open market rents

This is the conventional form of rent review clause. At regular intervals (normally no greater than every five years and sometimes less than five years) the rent is reviewed to that which would be obtained if the property was then let in the open market on a specified basis.

1.3.7 Combined clauses

With the increasing sophistication of rent review clauses, the parties may agree a clause combining different elements of the above, e.g. a clause providing for a rent to follow the RPI but with a provision to increase to the open market value subject to a specified cap.

1.3.8 Model forms of rent review

The Law Society and the Royal Institution of Chartered Surveyors have published model forms of rent review clauses. They are intended to provide 'some degree of standardisation' in order to assist the respective professions and their clients.

1.4 THE FORM OF A RENT REVIEW CLAUSE

The form of rent review clauses varies from lease to lease. A properly drafted clause will deal with most, if not all, of the following matters:

(a) starting the review;
(b) the direction of the review;
(c) the review machinery;

(d) time limits;
(e) notices and counter-notices;
(f) the valuation hypothesis;
(g) procedure;
(h) back payment of rent to the review date;
(i) interest; and
(j) documenting the review.

Each of these matters can give rise to litigation, as the cases in the following chapters show, if they are not drafted and dealt with carefully, clearly and unambiguously.

2
Construction of rent review clauses

2.1 THE ROLE OF THE COURT

Rent review clauses normally provide for the parties to agree the reviewed rent and, in default of agreement, for a surveyor to determine the rent acting either as an arbitrator or an expert. On the face of it therefore, the court has a limited role to play. There are however three broad situations where the court may become involved in the process of rent review.

- The first is where the machinery of the clause is in some way defective and the court is asked to rectify the clause or otherwise to cure the defect.
- The second is where the meaning of the clause is uncertain or disputed and the parties go to court asking for a ruling on what the clause means.
- The third is where, after the conclusion of the rent review, one party is dissatisfied and seeks relief from the court such as an appeal on a point of law under the *Arbitration Act* 1996 or to try to set aside an expert's determination or to sue an expert for negligence.

2.2 THE COURTS' GENERAL APPROACH

In the courts' consideration of rent review clauses three themes or principles recur. Firstly, a court construes the rent review clause having regard to its commercial purpose. Secondly, in considering the provisions of the clause dealing with valuation, the court applies what has been called a presumption of reality. Thirdly, these principles may be of limited application where the wording of the rent review clause is clear and has only one possible meaning. In that situation the court will normally apply the clear meaning. Cases illustrating each of these three themes or principles are considered below.

2.2.1 Having regard to the commercial purpose

Cases where the court has had regard to the commercial purpose of the clause include the following.

Law Land Company Ltd v Consumers' Association (1980)

The user clause in a lease provided that the premises were not to be used other than as offices of the Consumers' Association and its associated organisations. That user clause was to be incorporated in the hypothetical lease. The tenant argued that under the hypothetical lease the premises could only be let to it with the consequence that the rent would be low. The Court of Appeal rejected this argument holding that the lease before the Court was a commercial document and that the Court had to find a commercial solution to the problem. That solution was that the restriction should be taken to be read with the name of the hypothetical tenant.

British Gas Corporation v Universities Superannuation Scheme Ltd (1986)

A rent review clause required the revised rent to be assessed on the basis of a hypothetical lease 'containing the same provisions (other than as to the yearly rent) as are herein contained ...'. The lease provided for reviews every five years. The question arose whether in assessing the revised rent the valuer should assume a hypothetical letting incorporating rent reviews. The Court held that the clause should be construed so as to give effect to the basic purpose of the rent review clause and, in the absence of clear words to the contrary, a rent review clause should be construed as requiring future rent reviews to be taken into account in fixing the open market rental under the hypothetical letting. The Court said that 'there is really no dispute that the general purpose of a provision for rent review is to enable the landlord to obtain from time to time the market rental which the premises would command if let on the same terms on the open market at the review date. The purpose is to reflect the changes in the value of money and real increases in the value of the property during a long term.'

Basingstoke and Deane Borough Council v Host Group Ltd (1987)

In a lease of a public house for 99 years there were reviews to a 'reasonable current ground rent'. The Court of Appeal held that the hypothetical letting must be on the same terms (other than as to quantum of rent) as those subsisting in the actual lease. The Court said that in the absence of clear words or a special context indicating otherwise in a particular case the parties are to be taken as having intended that the notional letting postulated by their rent review clause is to be a letting on the same terms (other than as to quantum of rent) as those still subsisting between the parties in the actual existing lease. The parties are to be taken as having so intended because that would accord with, and give effect to, the general intention underlying the incorporation by them of a rent review clause in their lease.

In *Basingstoke and Deane* the Court of Appeal approved the approach in *British Gas* (above) and described the general approach to the construction of rent review clauses as follows.

> '... the valuer will be achieving the intended purpose ... if, but only if, he assesses the up-to-date rent on the same terms (other than as to quantum of rent) as the terms still subsisting between the parties under the actual, existing lease. If he departs from those terms, and assesses the up-to-date rent on the footing of terms materially less onerous to the tenant than those in the actual, existing lease, the rental at which he arrives will reflect, in addition to the rental increases attributable to a rise in property values or a fall in the value of money, an additional element, namely the increased rental attributable to the fact that he is calculating the rent of a lease on terms more favourable to the tenant than the terms in the actual, existing lease. Conversely, if he assesses the up-to-date rent on the basis of terms materially more onerous to the tenant than those in the actual existing lease, the rental figure at which the valuer arrives will not fully reflect the rise in property values or the fall in the value of money since the lease was granted or the rent was last fixed.'

2.2.2 The presumption of reality

The 'presumption of reality' applied by the courts is apparent from the passages above in *British Gas* and *Basingstoke and Deane*. The use of the presumption was made particularly clear in the 'headline' rent cases.

Co-operative Wholesale Society Ltd v National Westminster Bank plc (1995)

The Court of Appeal had to consider four different rent review clauses where the common issue was whether a 'headline' rent (see section 5.5) should be determined on review or whether deductions should be made to reflect concessionary or rent-free periods other than for fitting out. In three out of the four cases the Court held that a headline rent should not be determined. The Court applied a 'presumption of reality' that, in the absence of clear contrary words or necessary implication, it is to be assumed that the hypothetical letting is of the premises as they actually were, on the terms of the actual lease and in the circumstances as they actually existed with the result that a headline rent was not payable upon review. In the fourth case the Court held that the wording was so clear that the headline rent was payable.

2.2.3 Where the wording is clear and has only one possible meaning

In some cases the wording of the rent review clause will be so clear that it admits of only one possible meaning and there will be no room for the application of the presumption of reality or to have regard to the commercial purpose.

Pugh v Smith's Industries Ltd (1982)

A rent review clause provided for the reviewed rent to be the rent obtainable upon a letting on the terms of the lease but 'excluding therefrom the provisions of this clause'. It was held that the hypothetical lease was for a term without rent reviews. The wording was so clear that there was no room for any alternative reading.

MFI Properties Ltd v BICC Group Pension Trust Ltd (1986)

The Court referred to there being cases in which the language used by the parties showed beyond doubt that they intended an assumption for which, to a third party who knew nothing of the negotiations, no commercial purpose could be discerned. In such circumstances, the Court would have no option but to assume that it was a quid pro quo for some other concession in the course of negotiations. The Court could not reject it as absurd merely because it was counter-factual and had no outward commercial justification.

Beegas Nominees Ltd v Decco Ltd (2003)

A rent review clause in a lease of a distribution warehouse in a business park required the arbitrator to assume that the evidence of rental value of premises within two specified areas (each over 20 miles away) was evidence of rental value as if situated upon the business park. It was held that the clause required the arbitrator to make no allowance or discount for the different location of those two areas. The wording was clear and there was an express departure both from reality and from normal valuation practice to which the Court would give effect.

Canary Wharf Investments (Three) v Telegraph Group Ltd (2003)

A rent review clause assumed the letting of the premises 'for the grant thereof, the term of 25 years'. It was held that the natural meaning of the words was that the term ran from the date of the relevant rent review. The presumption of reality should not be mechanistically applied to rebut the natural reading to an ordinary commercial reader or to a property lawyer, particularly in light of the words 'for the grant thereof', which showed that the term was to run from the date of grant.

2.2.4 Application of these principles to rent review cases

There can be a tension or conflict between the above three principles when applied to individual rent review clauses. As appears from some of the cases considered later, apparently small differences in language can produce different results. In construing a rent review clause a court will, as with any other contract, have regard to the relevant factual background and apply the general principles of the construction of contracts.

Bank of Credit and Commercial International SA (In liquidation) v Ali (2002)

The general principles of construction were summarised by Lord Bingham in the House of Lords as follows.

> 'To ascertain the intention of the parties the court reads the terms of the contract as a whole, giving the words used their natural and ordinary meaning in the context of the agreement, the parties' relationship and all the relevant facts surrounding the transaction so far as known to the parties. To ascertain the parties' intentions the court does not of course inquire into the parties' subjective states of mind but makes an objective judgment based on the materials already identified.'

These general principles of construction apply to all contracts including leases and may help to resolve any tension or conflict between the above three principles.

3
The machinery of review

3.1 INTRODUCTION

The cases on rent review fall into two broad categories. Firstly, there are cases concerning the machinery or procedure for determining the reviewed rent. Secondly, there are cases concerning the ascertainment of the reviewed rent and in particular the terms of the hypothetical lease and the assumptions and disregards required for the valuation. This chapter deals with the first broad category and deals with the following topics. Chapter 4 deals with the second broad category.

- Initiating the review.
- The direction of the review.
- Deficiencies in the machinery of review.
- Time limits.
- Third party determination.
- When the reviewed rent is payable.
- Interest.
- Recording the review.

3.2 INITIATING THE REVIEW

There are a number of different ways in which the rent review may be started. Some review clauses provide for automatic reviews without the need for any notice. Others require notice, in differing degrees of formality, to be given. In some cases only the landlord may start the review, and in others both parties may do so. Where the clause refers to a step being taken 'in default of agreement', or some similar phrase, this does not normally require any prior attempt to agree.

Essoldo Ltd v Elcresta Ltd (1971)

A rent review clause provided for reference by the landlord to a third party 'in default of such agreement'. It was held that it was not a prerequisite of the landlord's right to ask for an appointment that there should have been an attempt to agree a rent before the date specified. The words meant 'in the absence of agreement'.

3.2.1 Formality of the initial notice

The degree of formality required of the initiating or trigger notice will depend upon the particular requirements of the rent review clause.

Dean & Chapter of Chichester Cathedral v Lennards Ltd (1977)

A rent review clause required notice in writing to be given to initiate the review. The notice was to state the suggested rent. The Court of Appeal held that the requirement to state the proposed rent was not mandatory but directory.

Shirlcar Properties Ltd v Heinitz (1983)

A letter to the tenant, stating the rent the landlord required under the heading 'subject to contract', was held to be an opening shot in negotiations and not a formal trigger notice.

Commission for New Towns v R Levy & Co Ltd (1990)

A rent review clause provided for the landlord to initiate the review by giving notice subject to the proviso that the 'rent review notice ... shall specify the yearly rent which [the landlord] proposes ...'. It was held that the proviso went to the essence of the contract and was not merely declaratory.

Patel v Earlspring Properties Ltd (1991)

A rent review clause required the tenant to serve within a specified period a counter-notice 'specifying the rent which the tenant is willing to pay from the relevant review date'. Time was of the essence. The tenant served a counter-notice within the specified period but failed to specify any figure. It was held by the Court of Appeal that the above provision was not mandatory and the counter-notice was valid.

3.2.2 Genuineness of the figure in the notice

Where the rent review clause requires the notice to specify a rent in the notice the courts have rejected the suggestion that the rent must be a genuine pre-estimate of the market rent. The position may be different if the notice is fraudulent as illustrated below by the non-rent-review case of *Rous v Mitchell.*

Davstone Holdings Ltd v Al-Rifai (1976)

A rent review notice specified a figure which it was very unlikely would have been determined to be the open market rental on the review date. It was held that this did not invalidate the notice although the position might have been different if the notice had contained a false and fraudulent expression of opinion as to the rental value.

Amalgamated Estates Ltd v Joystretch Ltd (1981)

A rent review clause provided for the landlord to give notice and the tenant to give a counter-notice, failing which the tenant should be deemed to have accepted the landlord's figure. The landlord gave notice but the tenant failed to serve a valid counter-notice. The Court of Appeal held that no term could be implied that the landlord's figure should be a bona fide and genuine pre-estimate of the open market rental value.

Rous v Mitchell (1991)

A landlord served a notice to quit on his tenant of an agricultural holding, alleging sublettings in breach of covenant. It was held that the notice to quit was vitiated by fraud (recklessness as to the truth of the allegations) and was therefore a nullity.

3.2.3 Notices electing for third party determination

Where a review clause requires that a notice or counter-notice shall elect for determination by a third party (time being of the essence for service of the notice), care needs to be taken in the preparation of the notice or counter-notice. In a number of the earlier cases the courts held that the language used was inadequate.

Bellinger v South London Stationers Ltd (1979)

A rent review clause provided for the rent to be determined 'at the election of the tenant to be made by counter-notice in writing' served by a specified date, time being of the essence. The tenant wrote a letter stating 'we do not accept your rent' which the Court held was not a valid counter-notice electing for third party determination.

Edlingham Ltd v MFI Furniture Centres Ltd (1981)

The rent review clause was in the same basic form as above. The tenant's letter stating 'will you please accept this letter as a counter-notice to the effect that we consider the rent of £50,000 is excessive' was held not to be an effective counter-notice electing for third party determination.

More recent cases suggest that the courts are taking a less strict and more pragmatic approach to such notices.

Nunes v Davies Laing & Dick Ltd (1986)

The rent review clause was in the same basic form as above. The tenant's letter referred to giving 'formal notice that the open market rental is £12,000 per annum' and calling on the landlord 'under the terms of the Lease to agree this'. It was held that the notice was in sufficiently clear terms to bring home to the ordinary landlord that the tenant was pursuing his right to elect third party determination.

Glofield Properties Ltd v Morley (No. 1) (1988)

In a lease with the same basic form of rent review clause, a letter asking that it be accepted 'as formal objection and counter-notice' was held to be a valid counter-notice.

Barrett Estate Services Ltd v David Greig (Retail) Ltd (1991)

Again in a lease with the same basic form, a tenant's letter acknowledging the landlord's figure and stating 'which I consider to be excessive' was held to be a valid counter-notice.

Lancecrest Ltd v Dr Ganiyu Asiwaju (2005)

The rent review clause in question provided that, upon the landlords serving the tenant with a valid notice of review, the tenant could contest the proposed new rent by serving a counter-notice 'informing the Landlords that the Tenant [does] not accept the annual amount proposed' within two months (time being of the essence).

The tenant received a notice of review from the landlords in February 2002. He replied in March 2002 contending that the notice was out of time and thus invalid. He refused to enter into arbitration. An independent surveyor subsequently determined the revised rent following submissions from the landlords. A County Court judge held that the landlords' notice was valid and that the tenant's response was not a valid counter-notice under the lease, since it did not challenge the new basic rent but rather the respondent's right to review the rent at all.

The Court of Appeal held that the tenant had served a valid counter-notice. It was in terms that were sufficiently clear and unambiguous to leave the respondent in no doubt, as an ordinary landlord, that he was purporting to exercise his right to challenge the proposed basic new rent.

3.3 THE DIRECTION OF THE REVIEW

There are three main possible directions:

- upwards only;
- upwards and downwards; and

- reviews with a minimum floor below which the rent cannot fall.

3.3.1 Upwards only

Most rent review clauses operate in an upwards only direction due to:

- the strength of the landlord's negotiating position, and
- the desire of the landlord for certainty of income.

The upwards only review is achieved by providing that if the open market rental value on the review date is less than the passing rent, then the passing rent shall continue to be payable.

Brimicam Investments Ltd v Blue Circle Heating Ltd (1995)

The inclusion of the following wording had the effect of creating an upwards only review, namely 'If the surveyor comes to the conclusion that the current market value of the demised premises is less than the rent operative for the period preceding the relevant period of three years (hereinafter called "the current rent") the new rent shall nevertheless be the same as the current rent, and the decision of the surveyor shall so state.'

3.3.2 Upwards and downwards

In the case of this form of review clause the rent may go up or down. This form of review clause is unusual and may lead to the tenant having to pay an extra amount upon review for the benefit of the upwards and downwards clause.

GRE Compass Ltd v The Guild of Drapers (1994)

In this case, although only the landlord could initiate the rent review, it was held that the tenant could propose a new rent and if the landlord refused to agree the tenant could use a third party determination procedure. This procedure could have the effect of decreasing the rent.

Royal Bank of Scotland plc v Jennings (1997)

In the case of this particular upwards and downwards review, the implication to be gained from the lease as a whole and in particular the reddendum and rent review provisions was that there would be a rent review for each of the rental periods. If the landlord (being the only person who could apply to the President of the RICS) failed to apply, the Court would supplement the machinery.

Hemingway Realty Ltd v The Clothworkers' Company (2005)

A lease between the claimant tenants and the defendant landlords, provided that 'the lessor shall have the right to review the yearly rent' in 1982 and every seven years thereafter. Since 1989, the landlords had chosen not to initiate any reviews. The tenants sought a review in 2003 on the basis that it might lead to a decrease in the yearly rent. The landlords contended that under the lease they alone had the right to initiate a review, and therefore that they could maintain the passing rent by declining to exercise this right. The tenants claimed that such a construction would run contrary to the purpose of a rent review clause, and would allow the landlords to convert what was in terms an open review clause into an upwards only rent review simply by refusing to allow the rent review to take place. They accordingly contended that the right to review was intended to be mutual.

Patten J dismissed the claim. There was no presumption that a rent review clause, even one incorporating an open review, ought to be exercisable by both parties. It would depend upon the form of review that the parties had chosen to incorporate. This could vary from a right to review that was exercisable by the landlord alone to a mandatory review on each of the review dates. There was no presumption either way.

In the present case, the lease provided in clear terms that the right to review the rent was exercisable only by the landlords. Accordingly, the absence of an upwards-only review formula was not sufficient to require or permit the court to construe the clause as requiring either a mandatory review or one that was exercisable by both the landlords and the tenants. Effect had to be given to the plain and obvious meaning of the rent review clause. This clearly gave the landlords the exclusive right to initiate a review, and they were entitled to take advantage of that.

3.3.3 Reviews with a minimum floor below which the rent cannot fall

In the case of this form of review there is a level below which the rent may not fall.

Barclays Bank plc v Savile Estates Ltd (2002)

A lease for 42 years provided for the rent to be reviewed at seven-year intervals. The reviewed rent was to be not less than the initial rent. The Court of Appeal held that this was not a true upwards only rent review clause but instead provided for upwards or downwards reviews with a minimum floor.

Addin Investments Ltd v Secretary of State for the Environment (1997)

A lease provided for the rent upon review to be the higher of £148,500 or the current open market value. It was held that the lease did not give the landlord an option to initiate a rent review but the proper construction was that there would be a rent review with the result that the rent could go up and down but not below £148,500.

3.4 DEFICIENCIES IN THE MACHINERY OF REVIEW

Where there are deficiencies in the machinery of review (other than those relating to time limits) the court will normally try to find a way to enable the review to take place.

Sudbrook Trading Estate Ltd v Eggleton (1981)

An option to buy the freehold reversion provided for the value to be ascertained by two valuers, one appointed by each party. One party refused to appoint a valuer. The House of Lords held that a deficiency in the machinery should not be allowed to defeat the option and that the Court itself should make an inquiry into the value of the freehold.

Royal Bank of Scotland plc v Jennings (1997)

A rent review clause provided for upwards and downwards reviews. The machinery only provided for the landlord to appoint an expert. The Court of Appeal held that there was a contract between the parties for a reviewed rent to be ascertainable and that if the landlord failed to make an appointment the Court could substitute its own machinery.

3.5 TIME LIMITS

3.5.1 The general rule that time is not of the essence

Some rent review clauses specify dates or time limits by which certain steps must be taken. For example, a landlord's trigger notice may have to be served not later than a certain date. The question arises whether time is of the essence in relation to such time limits. If time is of the essence and the relevant step is taken outside the time limit then that step will normally be invalid.

The general rule in relation to time limits in a rent review clause is that they are not of the essence.

United Scientific Holdings Ltd v Burnley Borough Council (1977)

The landlord failed to comply with a time limit in the rent review clause. The House of Lords held that, in the absence of any contraindications in the express words of the lease or the interrelationship of the rent review clause itself and other clauses or in the surrounding circumstances, the presumption is that the timetable specified in the review clause is not of the essence of the contract.

Weller v Akehurst (1981)

Where time is of the essence and one party has failed to comply with a time limit, the Court has no power to determine the reviewed rent itself even where the formula used is sufficiently clear to enable the court to do so. The review clause is inoperative where there has been a failure to operate according to its terms and time is of the essence.

Mere delay, however lengthy, does not destroy a landlord's right to review and the right to review cannot be abandoned in the sense of a unilateral indication of an intention not to exercise the right to review.

Amherst v James Walker Goldsmith & Silversmith Ltd (No. 2) (1983)

The rent review date in a lease was 24 June 1975 but the notice was not given until 10 May 1979. The tenant contended that the right to review had been lost due to the delay. It was held that the mere delay did not affect the landlord's right to a review.

3.5.2 Exceptions to the general rule that time is not of the essence

There are various exceptions to the general rule, which can be summarised as follows:

- where the parties expressly agree that time shall be of the essence;
- where the wording of the clause shows that the parties intended the time limits to be strict;
- where there are contraindications in the lease;
- where the parties provide for the consequence of non-compliance with a time limit; and
- where the review clause contains deeming provisions the effect of which is to make time of the essence.

These exceptions are considered below.

3.5.2.1 Express statements that time is of the essence

Where the parties expressly state that time is of the essence then the relevant time limit must be strictly complied with.

Amherst v James Walker Goldsmith & Silversmith Ltd (No. 1) (1980)

A rent review clause provided for time limits for doing three things:

(1) the landlord making an assessment of the reviewed rent by 25 December 1974;
(2) the parties agreeing the reviewed rent by a specified date; and
(3) the appointment of an independent surveyor by a specified date.

Time was stated to be of the essence of the second and third things but not of the first. It was held that time was of the essence for the second and third things but not the first.

Bradley (C) & Sons Ltd v Telefusion Ltd (1981)

A statement that 'time to be of the essence of this provision' was held to make time of the essence for the arbitrator to make his award.

Art & Sound Ltd v West End Litho Ltd (1992)

The arbitrator was required to make his award within a certain period, time being of the essence of that period. It was held that the review lapsed because the arbitrator did not make his award within the period.

London & Manchester Assurance Co Ltd v GA Dunn & Co (1983)

A requirement for a tenant's counter-notice to be given three months after the landlord's notice 'time to be of the essence hereof' was held by the Court of Appeal to apply only to the counter-notice and not to the landlord's notice. The Court said that an express provision for time to be of the essence of a particular time stipulation is an indication that time was not intended to be of the essence for other time stipulations.

3.5.2.2 Where the wording of the clause shows an intention that time limits are strict

In some cases the use of emphatic language has been held to make time limits strict, as a matter of necessary implication from the language used by the parties.

Drebbond v Horsham District Council (1978)

Time was held to be of the essence where notice had to be served on or before a particular date 'but not otherwise'.

Chelsea Building Society v R & H Millett (1994)

This review clause provided that 'It shall be a condition precedent' to the determination of the reviewed rent that notice be given by a particular date. The Court held that these words made time of the essence.

First Property Growth Partnership LP v Royal & Sun Alliance Property Services Ltd (2003)

The Court held that the words 'but not at any other time' made time of the essence for service of a trigger notice.

These cases must be contrasted with other cases where it has been held that similar wording does not make time of the essence.

Printing House Properties Ltd v JW Winston & Co Ltd (1982)

The landlord was required to serve a trigger notice during the fourth year for a review at the end of that year of a seven-year term but did not serve it until just after the end of the fifth year. It was held that time was not of the essence and the landlord had not lost his right to a review.

Touche Ross & Co v Secretary of State for the Environment (1983)

The Court of Appeal held that time was not of the essence of a provision requiring reference to a surveyor 'so soon as practicable and in any event not later than three months' after service of the landlord's trigger notice.

Thorn EMI Pension Trust Ltd v Quintin Hazell plc (1984)

A rent review clause required that 'the question of what is a fair market rack rental of the demised premises shall as soon as practicable ... be referred for the decision to a surveyor'. It was held that the language was not distinguishable from that in *Touche Ross* and that time was not of the essence.

McDonald's Property Company Ltd v HSBC Bank plc (2001)

The Court held that a mechanism which envisaged that the reviewed rent would be determined either by agreement or by an expert 'not less than fourteen days before the review date' was insufficient to make time of the essence.

3.5.2.3 Contraindications in the review clause

Apart from the language used in the clause there may be other indications in the review clause which indicate that time was not intended to be of the essence.

Kirkland Properties Ltd v GRA Developments Ltd (1978)

The landlord had different successive rights to seek rent reviews, each for a different date. It was held that each particular right superseded previous rights for which time was therefore of the essence.

H Turner & Son Ltd v Confederated Life Insurance Co (UK) Ltd (2003)

A rent review clause provided for the landlord to serve a late notice if it should have failed or neglected to serve a notice by a specified date. It was held that this clause made time of the essence for service of the notice by the specified date and that if a late notice was served the increased rent only took effect after the service of the late notice.

Lancecrest Ltd v Dr Ganiyu Asiwaju (2005)

The lease in question provided that the landlords had the 'option' of a rent review with effect from the end of every fourth year of the lease period. This was exercisable by giving the tenant notice of a review 'no more than 12 months before the review date', stating the new basic rent. The tenant could contest the proposed new rent by serving a counter-notice within two months, time being of the essence.

The landlords acquired the reversion to the lease in August 2001, six months after the first review date on 5 February 2001, when no trigger notice had been served. On 19 February 2002, the landlords gave the tenant notice proposing a new basic rent from 1 February 2001.

The landlords accepted that on a true construction of the rent review clause their notice should have been served on or before 5 February 2001, but contended that it was nonetheless valid since time was not of the essence of that date. The tenant submitted that the 54-week lateness rendered the notice invalid.

The Court of Appeal held that the landlords' notice was valid. It was settled principle following *United Scientific Holdings v Burnley BC* (1978) that, in the absence of any contraindications in the lease or surrounding circumstances, the presumption was that the timetable specified in a rent review clause for determining the rent payable in the period following the review date was not of the essence of the contract. The fact that the parties had described the rent review as an 'option' for the landlord did not mean that it was to be treated as an option in the legal sense, with the consequence that time was of the essence of any stipulation as to its implementation. The fact that time was made expressly of the essence for the service of the counter-notice did not mean that time was to be impliedly of the essence for the service of the landlords' trigger notice.

3.5.2.4 Contraindications in the lease

There may also be contraindications in the lease which show that time is of the essence. The classic example of this is where the tenant has a right to break exercisable at a date linked to the rent review date. In such a case, time may be held to be of the essence. The reasons for this are, first, that the time limits for exercising an option are mandatory and so the parties must be taken to have intended that the same should apply to the rent review and, secondly, that the tenant will need to seek advice on the level of rent or know what rent may be payable before making the decision whether or not to exercise the break clause.

C Richards & Son Ltd v Karenita Ltd (1971)

A rent review clause provided that the landlord could review the rent at the end of the seventh year of the term by giving notice at any time during the first three months of the seventh year of the term. The tenant had the right to break the lease at the end of the seventh year by giving three months' notice. It was held that time was of the essence for service of the landlord's rent review notice and that a notice given in the eighth month of the year was out of time and invalid.

Al Saloom v Shirley James Travel Services Ltd (1981)

The same result was reached where the last day for serving the landlord's notice for review was the same as the last day for serving a tenant's notice to break.

Coventry City Council v J Hepworth & Son Ltd (1983)

A lease for 42 years contained a tenant's break clause under which notice had to be served by 30 September 1974. There was also a rent review clause under which the landlord's rent review notice had to be served by 31 December 1973 and a single arbitrator or two arbitrators appointed by 31 March 1974 or 30 April 1974 respectively. The landlord failed to serve his rent review notice by 31 December 1973 and it was held that time was of the essence for service of that notice with the result that the right to a review was lost.

Legal & General Assurance (Pension Management) Ltd v Cheshire County Council (1984)

Notice under both a rent review clause and a tenant's break clause in a lease were operative at the same dates on service of not less than six months' notice. It was held that time was of the essence for service of the rent review notice.

Central Estates Ltd v Secretary of State for the Environment (1997)

A lease contained a break clause exercisable at the end of the first 21 years by the tenant giving six months' notice. It also contained provision for a rent review at the end of the same period by either party giving not less than 12 months' notice. It was held that time was of the essence for service of the rent review notice due to the correlation between the break clause and the rent review provisions.

These cases must be contrasted with ones where the interrelationship between the two clauses was less precise and time was held not to be of the essence in the rent review clause.

Edwin Woodhouse Trustees Co Ltd v Sheffield Brick Co plc (1984)

In this case the review clause contained no precise timetable but provided for an automatic review which either party could initiate. The Court held that there was not sufficient interrelationship between the rent review clause and the break clause to make time of the essence for the review clause.

Metrolands Investments Ltd v JH Dewhurst Ltd (1986)

In this case the event in respect of which time was of the essence was the arbitrator's award, which had to be obtained by 18 August 1981. The tenant had a break clause operable by notice given between 19 August 1981 and 18 November 1981. It was held that time was not of the essence because:

- the event as to which time was of the essence was outside the landlord's control; and
- the tenant could mitigate the potential hardship by setting the arbitration in motion.

3.5.2.5 When the parties provide for the consequences of non-compliance with a time limit

Where the parties have provided not only for a particular step to be taken within a specified time but also have expressly provided for the consequences in the event of default, then this provides an indication that time may be of the essence. The weight to be attached to this indication will vary depending upon the nature of the default provisions. A default clause which merely expresses what would be implied anyway may carry little weight, whereas one which provides for a result that would not normally be implied may carry greater weight and may in some circumstances be decisive. The difference appears from the cases considered below.

Lewis v Barnett (1982)

A rent review clause provided that, in the event of the landlord failing to make application for the appointment of a surveyor within a specified period, the rent review notice was to be 'void and of no effect'. It was held by the Court of Appeal that a failure to apply in time made the rent review notice void and invalidated the whole procedure.

Mammoth Greeting Cards Ltd v Agra Ltd (1990)

A rent review clause provided that if the tenant did not serve counter-notice within two months, the rent should be conclusively fixed at the amount stated in the landlord's notice. It was held that time was of the essence and a tenant's counter-notice served out of time was of no effect. The word 'conclusively fixed' were so strongly suggestive of finality that the only conclusion was that time was of the essence.

Banks v Kokkanos (1999)

A rent review clause provided that if the rent had not been agreed and the landlord had not applied for the appointment of a valuer by a certain date, then the tenant could serve a notice specifying a rent which would become the reviewed rent unless the landlord applied for an appointment within three months. It was held that time was impliedly of the essence and the rent was that in the tenant's notice when the landlord failed to apply within the specified time.

Iceland Frozen Foods plc v Dangoor (2002)

A rent review clause provided that if the landlord should neglect to make an application to the President of the RICS, any notice already given by the landlord should be 'void and of no effect'. However there was no date specified by which the application had to be made to the President. It was held that the provision did not make time of the essence for the application to the President.

3.5.2.6 Review clauses containing deeming provisions

The cases on deeming provisions provide another example of the principle just considered, i.e. where the parties provide for the consequence of non-compliance with a time limit. A deeming provision will typically provide that if, say, the tenant fails to serve a counter-notice within a specified period 'the tenant shall be deemed to have agreed to pay the rent specified in the landlord's notice'.

Henry Smith's Charity Trustees v AWADA Trading & Promotions Ltd (1984)

A rent review clause provided a timetable for:

- the service of a landlord's trigger notice specifying the new rent;
- a tenant's counter-notice stating the tenant's proposed rent; and
- in the event of disagreement, for the landlord to apply to the President of the RICS.

Each step had to be taken within a specified period and if the step was not taken in that time the rent was deemed to be the amount in, as the case may be, the landlord's notice or the tenant's counter-notice. The landlord failed to apply to the President of the RICS within the specified time. It was held that due to the deeming provisions time was of the essence for this step and the rent was that specified in the tenant's counter-notice.

Mecca Leisure Ltd v Renown Investments (Holdings) Ltd (1984)

A rent review clause provided for the landlord to serve a trigger notice and the tenant to serve a counter-notice objecting within one month, failing which the rent was that specified in the landlord's notice. The tenant failed to give a counter-notice within time. It was held that time was not of the essence and that the deeming provision did not make time of the essence.

This case must now be read in the light of *Starmark* below where the reasoning in *Mecca* was disapproved.

Starmark Enterprises Ltd v CPL Distribution Ltd (2002)

A rent review clause provided for the landlord to initiate the review by serving a rent notice providing for the increase of rent. If the tenant failed to serve a counter-notice within a specified period it was 'deemed to have agreed to pay the increased rent specified in the Rent Notice'. The Court of Appeal held that the deeming provision made time of the essence. The deeming provision was not simply part of the administrative procedure or machinery but was an essential part of the contract which would not be rewritten by the Court. The Court held that *Mecca Leisure* was wrongly decided.

3.5.3 Making time of the essence

When a rent review clause contains time limits for particular steps to be taken by only one party (usually the landlord) but time is not of the essence, the other party (usually the tenant) may be able to serve a notice making time of the essence.

However in order for the tenant to serve such a notice there must be, first, a time limit and, second, no procedure for the tenant to take that step.

Factory Holdings Group Ltd v Leboff International Ltd (1987)

A rent review clause provided for an arbitrator to be appointed by the President of the RICS upon the application of either party. The tenant gave 28 days purported notice to the landlord to make time of the essence for application to the President and the landlord applied outside that time. It was held that the notice was ineffective as the step was one which the tenant could have taken.

Barclays Bank plc v Savile Estates Ltd (2002)

The Court of Appeal held that in the case of a rent review clause requiring the landlord to apply to the President of the RICS there was an implied term on the landlord to apply within a reasonable time and that the tenant could serve a notice making time of the essence in relation to that step.

Northern & Midland Holdings v Magnet Ltd (2004)

The rent review provisions in two leases provided that if the landlord and tenant failed to agree the open market rental value before the 'appropriate date', it would be determined by an independent surveyor. If a surveyor could not be agreed upon by both parties, an appointment would be made by the President of the RICS 'upon the application of the landlord at any time after the appropriate date'.

In the 1999 rent review, there was no agreement before the 'appropriate date' of 29 September 1999. In June 2001, after lengthy but unsuccessful negotiations, the tenant's surveyor wrote to the landlord requiring that an independent surveyor be appointed and that the application be made to the President by 4 July 2001. They further stated that time was to be of the essence. The landlord did not, however, apply to the President until December 2001. A surveyor was subsequently appointed in respect of each property. The tenant contended that the landlord was no longer entitled to pursue a rent review owing to its failure to comply with the July deadline. The landlord sought a declaration that the appointment of the surveyor was valid.

Mann J allowed the claim. Although the landlord was entitled to apply to the President 'at any time after the appropriate date', there had to be some limit to the time within which it could take that step. Otherwise, the landlord would be able to do so a considerable time after the rent review period, and even after the end of the lease, which would make little or no commercial sense. The key issue was the extent of this limit. His Lordship held that it was an implied term of the lease that the the landlord's reference to the President should be made within a 'reasonable time' of a failure to agree on the identity of a surveyor.

It was not possible to make time of the essence until the 'reasonable time' had passed. In the present case, there had been no attempt to agree upon a surveyor before the tenant's June letters and so the 'reasonable time' had not even begun when those letters were served. Accordingly, the tenant had not been entitled to make time of the essence in the letters.

3.5.4 Applications under section 12 of the *Arbitration Act* 1996

Before the *Arbitration Act* 1996 (the '1996 Act') was enacted it was sometimes possible, where the lease provided for reference to arbitration to apply to court under section 27 of the *Arbitration Act* 1950, for an extension of time for the service of a notice or counter-notice. That option is unlikely to be available under the present provision, now section 12(1) of the 1996 Act, as it only applies to 'some step to begin arbitral proceedings'. It is unlikely that a trigger notice or a counter-notice in a rent review clause is such a step. This view is consistent with the approach of the Departmental Advisory Committee on Arbitration Law (DAC) chaired by Lord Saville which led to the 1996 Act. The DAC concluded that it was desirable to make it more difficult to obtain extensions of time for references to arbitration. Section 12(1) also applies to a step to begin 'other dispute resolution procedures which must be exhausted before arbitral proceedings can be begun' (section 12(1)(b)). This may be apt to include the service of a landlord's rent review trigger notice.

There is another difficulty with both the above limbs, which is the criteria applied under section 12(3). Under that subsection the court shall make an order extending time only if satisfied:

'(a) that the circumstances are such as were outside the reasonable contemplation of the parties when they agreed the procedures in question and that it would be just to extend the time, or
(b) that the conduct of one party makes it unjust to hold the other party to the strict terms of the provision in question.'

The indications in the cases so far are that (a) will be hard to establish.

Fox & Widley v Guram (1998)

A tenant failed to give a counter-notice requiring arbitration in time as a result of which the rent was to be reviewed to that specified in the landlord's notice. The tenant applied for an extension of time under section 12 on the grounds:

(a) that the rent specified in the landlord's notice was excessive; and
(b) of certain correspondence passing between the parties, said to have led the tenant to think that it did not have to serve a counter-notice.

The Court refused to grant an extension of time under either section 12(3)(a) or (b).

Harbour and General Works Ltd v The Environment Agency (2000)

In a construction dispute under the ICE conditions one party failed to refer the matter to arbitration within the specified terms. The Court refused to grant an extension of time stressing that the DAC and section 12 marked a clear change in the law and practice relating to the extension of time for commencement of an arbitration beyond the time specified in a contractual time-bar provision.

Monella v Pizza Express (Restaurants) Ltd (2004)

The landlord missed the time limit for applying for the appointment of an arbitrator. It applied for an extension of time under section 12 arguing that the change of law in *Starmark* was outside the reasonable contemplation of the parties to the lease when they agreed the relevant provisions. The Court rejected the application holding that:

- a change in the law was certainly not unlikely; and
- the change in the law did not contribute to the landlord's failure to effect a reference.

The Court said that the fact that a party might not give notice in time, for whatever reason, is a fact of commercial life which would readily have been contemplated when the lease was granted.

3.6 THIRD PARTY DETERMINATION

It is normal for a rent review clause to provide for a third party to determine the reviewed rent if the parties cannot agree. In the absence of a provision dealing with what is to happen if the parties cannot agree the court will provide the machinery for determining the rent. If necessary, the court itself would determine the rent.

It is also normal for rent review clauses to provide expressly whether the third party is to act as an expert or an arbitrator. If the clause does not do so it is a question of construction whether the third party is an expert or an arbitrator.

Safeway Food Stores Ltd v Banderway Ltd (1983)

A rent review clause provided for an umpire to settle the question. It was held that the umpire was to act as an independent expert as the issue was one of expertise and, in contrast to other provisions in the lease, there was no reference to the *Arbitration Act* 1950.

The differences between an expert and an arbitrator are considered at length in the RICS guidance note for *Surveyors Acting as Arbitrators and as Independent Experts in Commercial Property Rent Reviews* (8th edition). In the case of determination by an expert, it is difficult to set that determination aside and a disappointed party will be left to try to pursue a claim in negligence against the expert. In the case of an arbitrator there are limited powers given to the courts to interfere with awards in the case of error of law or serious irregularity. These matters are considered in more detail in later chapters.

The courts will only interfere with the appointment of a third party by the RICS where the President has departed from his instructions by appointing someone who does not fulfil the criteria in the lease. Where the criteria require the exercise of the President's expertise, he will only have departed from his instructions if his decision is unreasonable.

Epoch Properties Ltd v British Homes Stores (Jersey) Ltd (2004)

Under a lease of retail premises in Jersey, if the parties could not agree upon an independent chartered surveyor to determine the reviewed rent, the appointment was to be made by the President of the RICS. The lease required a surveyor with experience of similar or comparable premises, and provided that a mainland surveyor could only be appointed if there was no suitably experienced surveyor in the Channel Islands.

The landlord and tenant disagreed as to whether the property should be classified as a 'prime retail store' or a 'variety store', for which different valuation methods applied. In the absence of agreement on a surveyor, the tenant applied to the President. The tenant stated that the property was a variety store, as to which there was no chartered surveyor in Jersey with the required experience, and asked for a mainland surveyor. The President informed the landlord of this application but did not enclose copies of the tenant's correspondence. The landlord replied that the expert should be Jersey-based.

The President agreed with the tenant and appointed a mainland surveyor. The landlord sought a declaration that the appointment was contrary to the lease and therefore invalid.

The Court of Appeal, Channel Islands held that the correct approach to assessing the validity of the President's appointment was to view his role as that of an expert: if he asks the right questions and exercises his jurisdiction accordingly, his decision cannot be challenged. Accordingly:

(i) Where a lease lays down criteria for the appointment, these must be satisfied. If the President departs from his instructions by appointing someone who does not fulfil the criteria his decision is invalid.
(ii) Where the criteria require the exercise of the President's expertise, he will not be found to have departed from his instructions unless he has reached a decision which no reasonable President would have made.

The President's categorisation of the premises as a variety store and subsequent conclusion that the appointee had the required experience were not unreasonable. His decision was not vitiated by his failure to send copies of the tenant's representations to the landlord. Upon receiving an application from one party to a lease to exercise his power of appointment, the President is merely required to notify the other party of that fact: there is no requirement for an oral hearing or prolonged written interchange. It was sufficient that the landlord had the opportunity of putting its case to the President.

3.7 WHEN THE REVIEWED RENT IS PAYABLE

It is normal for a rent review clause to provide expressly for the date from which the reviewed rent is payable. The date will invariably be the review date rather than the date from which the reviewed rent is determined. If there is no express provision the court is likely to hold that the rent is payable from the review date.

Bailey (CH) Ltd v Memorial Enterprises Ltd (1974)

A rent review clause provided for a review on 21 September 1969 but did not state from when the rent was payable. The reviewed rent was determined by an arbitrator in March 1973 and at first instance the Court held that rent was payable from that date. The Court of Appeal reversed this part of the decision and held that the rent was payable as from 21 September 1969.

Where the reviewed rent is not determined until after the review, the rent review clause will normally provide for a balancing sum to be paid. If the clause does not specify when this balancing sum is to be paid then it will be payable on the next quarter day after determination.

South Tottenham Land Securities Ltd v R & A Millet (Shops) Ltd (1984)

A lease provided for a rent review on 25 March 1980. An arbitrator was appointed and his award taken up by the landlord in November 1980. On 25 November 1980 the landlord forfeited the lease for non-payment of the increased rent due for the June and September 1980 quarter. It was held that the forfeiture was premature and unlawful because the obligation to pay the rent did not arise until the quarter day next following the award, i.e. 25 December 1980.

3.8 INTEREST

Rent review clauses often provide for the payment of interest on any balancing sum which is payable where the reviewed rent is determined after the review date. In the absence of such a provision there is no implied term that interest is payable on the balancing sum.

Trust House Forte Albany Hotels Ltd v Daejan Investments Ltd (1980)

The landlord contended that a term was to be implied into the rent review clause that if the reviewed rent was not determined by the date from which it was payable, interest was payable. It was held that it was not necessary to give business efficacy to the rent review clause to imply such a term and therefore no such term was to be implied.

However, in an arbitration the arbitrator may have power to award interest under section 49 of the *Arbitration Act* 1996 which provides that, in the absence of agreement, the arbitrator may award simple or compound interest from such dates, at such rates and with such rests as meet the justice of the case on the whole or part of any amount awarded. By section 49(5) an amount awarded includes an amount payable in consequence of a declaratory award.

3.9 RECORDING THE REVIEW

The rent review clause will normally provide for recording the reviewed rent by way of, for example, a memorandum endorsed on the lease. It may be important to follow this procedure to ensure that the review is concluded and no further review can take place.

Esso Petroleum Co Ltd v Anthony Gibbs Financial Services Ltd (1982)

The surveyors for a landlord and tenant took the view that there was no increase in the rent for office premises but did not formally agree this or endorse any memorandum on the lease. The landlord then sought to invoke the review. It was held that there was no binding agreement between the surveyors and that the landlord was entitled to invoke the review.

4
The property to be valued

4.1 THE PROPERTY

The presumption of reality requires that in the absence of clear contrary words or necessary implication, it is assumed that the hypothetical letting is of the premises as they actually were at the review date.

Ponsford v HMS Aerosols Ltd (1979)

The review clause required the tenant to pay 'a reasonable rent for the demised premises'.

It was held that the premises would have included the improvements without express provision to that effect, on the principle that anything made part of the premises by the tenants enures to the landlord.

Co-operative Wholesale Society Ltd v National Westminster Bank plc (1995)

'In the absence of clear contrary words or necessary implication, it is assumed that the hypothetical letting required by the clause is of the premises as they actually were, on the terms of the actual lease and in the circumstances as they actually existed.'

4.2 NOTIONAL PREMISES

The rent may have to be assessed by reference to notional premises different in some way from the demised premises, but the notional premises will possess the attributes of the demised premises save as directed otherwise.

Dukeminster (Ebbgate House One) Ltd v Somerfield Property Co Ltd (1997)

The demised premises were a retail distribution centre of some 250,000 square feet on an industrial estate at Ross-on-Wye. The lessor was entitled to elect that the rent should be reviewed to 82.5% of the market rent of notional premises applied as a rent per square foot to the demised premises. The notional premises were defined as 'a warehouse unit within a 35-mile radius of Ross-on-Wye and having the following characteristics: (a) a total gross internal area of 50,000 square feet.'

The lessor elected to have the rent reviewed by reference to the notional premises, but this gave rise to the difficulty that within a 35-mile radius there were a wide variety of rental levels in different locations. The landlord contended that it was entitled to elect where the notional premises were situated.

It was held by the Court of Appeal that the Court had to find a commercial solution to the problem posed so as not to produce a valuation, whether it be too high or too low, which cannot reasonably have been intended to apply to the actual premises.

The reason for reviewing the rent by reference to notional premises was that at the date of the lease there were no comparables as large as the demised premises in the area. The solution was to 'gear' the rent on review to the rent payable in respect of a smaller warehouse of 50,000 sq ft in relation to which there was, and would be, no difficulty in finding suitable comparables; but there were no 50,000 sq ft warehouses to speak of in the immediate vicinity of Ross-on-Wye. There would be no difficulty in finding them within a 35-mile radius.

Given that there would inevitably be substantial variations in rental values in such an area, the Court concluded that it could only reasonably have been intended that the notional warehouse should be situated in a location comparable to the site of the premises in Ross-on-Wye.

Beegas Nominees Ltd v Decco Ltd (2003)

The demised premises were a distribution warehouse of some 110,000 sq ft at Stone Business Park, Staffordshire. At the time of the lease, Stone Business Park was relatively undeveloped compared with similar business parks in Tamworth and Minworth. It was provided that in determining the market value at rent review:

> 'The Landlord and the Tenant agree that and the Surveyor is required to assume that evidence of rental value of premises (comprising buildings and ancillary areas) which are being used for or may lawfully be used for purposes within Class B1 or Class B8 or both of the *Town and Country Planning (Use Classes) Order* 1987 either which are of at least 50,000 square feet measured gross internal and which are located in or within a five mile radius of Tamworth, Staffordshire or in or within a five mile radius of Minworth, Birmingham is evidence of Market Rental Value of the Premises as if those premises were situated upon the Stone Business Park.'

The tenant contended, on the basis of the decision in *Dukeminster*, that although the arbitrator could have regard to comparable properties in Tamworth and Minworth as evidence of rental value, he was not precluded from discounting them on account of location.

It was held that, if the tenant were right, the quoted provision would serve no useful purpose. The arbitrator could not discount values of comparable properties at Tamworth or Minworth on account of location.

4.3 ASSUMED COMPLIANCE WITH REPAIRING COVENANTS

The premises are to be valued in their actual condition, but the tenant is assumed to have complied with his repairing covenants because otherwise he would profit from his own wrong.

Family Management v Gray (1980)

The tenant had failed to comply with his repairing covenants on the expiry of his business lease, for which the landlords claimed damages. Damages for dilapidations could not, under section 13 of the *Landlord and Tenant Act* 1927 (the '1927 Act'), exceed the amount by which the value of the reversion had diminished. In the meantime, a new lease was in the process of being agreed under section 13 of the *Landlord and Tenant Act* 1954 (the '1954 Act'), which provided the new rent payable would be 'that at which, having regard to the terms of the tenancy … the holding might reasonably be expected to be let in the open market by a willing lessor'.

The judge had calculated the damage to the reversion by reference to the decrease in the rental value of the premises with vacant possession on the open market in light of the dilapidations. The Court of Appeal overturned this decision, approving the landlords' submission that it was not right to ignore the operation of LTA 1954, section 34, under which the tenants:

> 'could not, in diminution of what was the proper rent to be paid, urge their own default in having failed to comply with the repairing covenants under the lease as a justification reason for a lower rent'.

Harmsworth Pension Funds Trustees v Charringtons Industrial Holdings (1985)

Waller J upheld the landlords' contention that, in determining the 'fair market yearly rack rent' for review purposes, any breach by the tenant of its covenant to repair should be disregarded. The Court of Appeal's finding to like effect in *Gray* in relation to new leases under the LTA 1954 was part of the *ratio* of that case and accordingly took precedence over possibly contrary *obiter dicta* in *Fawke v Viscount Chelsea* (1980). The landlord's right to damages for breach of the repairing covenant made no difference, since it would be of little or no value if the tenant was in financial difficulties.

Secretary of State for the Environment v Euston Centre Investments Ltd (No. 2) (1994)

The tenant appealed from the rent review arbitrator's decision that he had been obliged to remove asbestos from the premises prior to the review date and that there should be no change in the valuation to take account of the continuing need to remove it. Chadwick J held, following *Harmsworth*, that in determining the fair yearly market rent under the lease there should be disregarded any diminishing effect on such rent of the tenant's failure to repair the demised premises in breach of his obligations.

Land Securities plc v Westminster City Council (No. 2) (1995)

In an appeal against the decision of a rent review arbitrator, it was common ground between the parties that 'for the purposes of the rent review the tenants were to be assumed to have complied with all their obligations in the lease, including their repairing obligations'.

Gibson Investments Ltd v Chesterton plc (2003)

It was provided in the lease that the tenant was responsible for the repair, renewal or replacement of the air-conditioning system in the premises. The original system was inadequate. Of two alternative replacement systems, the tenant chose one which created more floor space by relocating various parts of the system.

Judge Rich QC accepted the tenant's submission that this constituted an improvement. It was, therefore, covered by the provision in the rent review clause that no account would be taken on such review of 'any effect or any improvement to the demised premises to which the landlord shall have given written consent'. Any increased value conferred by the new system would accordingly be disregarded if consent had been given, and the valuation would work on the assumption that the original repair clause had been met.

4.4 IMPROVEMENTS

4.4.1 Reasons for disregard

It is regarded as unfair that the tenant should pay rent for improvements he has carried out at his own expense.

Historic Houses Hotels Ltd v Cadogan Estates (1995)

The rent review clause provided that in determining the rent at review any alterations or improvements carried out by the lessee should be disregarded other than those pursuant to any obligation of the lessee and at the lessee's sole expense and with the previous consent in writing of the lessor. Various alterations and improvements were made to the premises with the lessor's licence. The relevant licences contained a covenant by the lessee that when the relevant works were completed all the covenants and provisions contained in the lease would be applicable to the premises in their altered state, as if the premises in that altered state had originally been comprised in the lease. The landlord contended that at review it had to be assumed that the premises were originally demised in their altered state and that the disregard in the rent review clause is excluded in relation to improvements covered by the licences.

It was held that the improvements were to be disregarded.

The obvious reason for the standard disregard for improvements was that if a lessee carries out improvements to the premises at his own expense which would benefit the landlord after the expiration of the lease, it would not be fair or reasonable that the tenant should pay rent on the value of the improvements for the rest of the lease.

The licences could not be construed as excluding the disregard for improvements. Very clear words would be required to achieve that result. It would have been unreasonable for the landlords to have insisted, as a condition of granting licence for an improvement, that the value of the improvement would not be disregarded at review.

4.4.2 **Section 34 of the *Landlord and Tenant Act* 1954**

Rent review clauses commonly incorporate by reference the terms of the disregard for improvements in section 34 of the *Landlord and Tenant Act* 1954.

As enacted, section 34, so far as material, read as follows:

' ... there being disregarded:

(a) any effect on rent of the fact that the tenant has or his predecessors in title have been in occupation of the holding,

(b) any goodwill attaching to the holding by reason of the carrying on thereat of the business of the tenant (whether by him or by a predecessor of his in that business),

(c) any effect on rent of any improvement carried out by the tenant or a predecessor in title of his otherwise than in pursuance of an obligation to his immediate landlord, ...'

Section 34 in its original form only required the disregard of improvements carried out during the current tenancy.

East Coast Amusement Co Ltd v British Transport Board (known as In re 'Wonderland', Cleethorpes) (1965)

The tenant was applying for a new lease under Part II of the *Landlord and Tenant Act* 1954. The question arose whether in determining the rent section 34(c) required certain improvements (carried out not under the current lease but a previous lease held by the same tenant) to be disregarded.

The House of Lords held that it did not. Section 34(c) referred only to improvements carried out by the tenant who was making the application for the tenancy, and effected during the term of the tenancy current when the application was made, or by a predecessor in title of his to the same tenancy.

Section 34 was accordingly amended in 1969 to read as follows:

... there being disregarded: ...

'(c) any effect on rent of an improvement to which this paragraph applies'

and the following subsection shall be added (the present section, as amended by the foregoing provisions, becoming subsection (1)):

'(2) Paragraph (c) of the foregoing subsection applies to any improvement carried out by a person who at the time it was carried out was the tenant, but only if it was carried out otherwise than in pursuance of an obligation to his immediate landlord, and either it was carried out during the current tenancy or the following conditions are satisfied, that is to say:

(a) that it was completed not more than twenty-one years before the application for the new tenancy was made; and
(b) that the holding or any part of it affected by the improvement has at all times since the completion of the improvement been comprised in tenancies of the description specified in section 23(1) of this Act; and
(c) that at the termination of each of those tenancies the tenant did not quit.'

Whether the rent review clause incorporates section 34 in its original form or as amended by the *Law of Property Act* 1969 depends on the wording of the lease.

Brett v Brett Essex Golf Club Ltd (1986)

The tenants were a golf club company. During the course of their original lease, granted in 1973, they laid out a nine-hole course on nearby land not then included in their demise. In 1978, this lease was surrendered and a new lease granted to the tenants which included the nine-hole course. This new lease, as rectified, included a rent review clause which provided for the disregard, in ascertaining the open market rent, of 'those matters set out in paragraphs (a), (b) and (c) of section 34 of the *Landlord and Tenant Act* 1954'. The questions which arose were whether the lease referred to section 34 in its original form or as amended, and whether the works carried out by the appellant company prior to the grant of the 1978 lease were to be disregarded.

It was held that the rent review clause incorporated the original form of section 34. The reference to paragraphs (a), (b) and (c) were not apt to refer to and include subsection (2) of the amended version. The incorporation of subsection (2) would require a considerable amount of imaginative construction, and the draftsman could be expected to have made provision for the necessary adaptation. Finally, other clauses referred to statutes as amended.

4.4.3 Improvements carried out before the lease was granted

Improvements carried out before the lease was granted are not to be disregarded as work carried out by the tenant unless carried out by the tenant in anticipation of and referable to the grant of the lease.

Brett v Brett Essex Golf Club Ltd (1986)

The facts are set out above.

It was held that the works were not to be disregarded, for two reasons. Firstly, the clubhouse and nine-hole course were included in the definition of the demised premises, and their construction could not be regarded as improvements to the demised premises. Secondly, the work was not carried out by the company as tenant under the 1978 lease.

Hambros Bank Executor & Trustee Co Ltd v Superdrug Stores Ltd (1985)

The defendant tenant was granted a lease dated 15 September 1976 with a rent review every five years. There was a disregard of 'any effect on rent of any improvement carried out by the Tenant'. The 'tenant' meant Superdrug Stores Ltd. They were allowed into possession before the lease was granted to carry out improvements. The landlords argued that these improvements should not be disregarded, on the ground that when they were carried out the prospective tenants were not yet 'the tenant' within the meaning of the clause.

It was held that the improvements in question fell to be disregarded. The decisions, dicta and principles expressed in the *Brett* and *Wonderland* cases were not applicable to the present case in which the improvements had been carried out shortly before the current tenancy by the person soon to become the current tenant and with a view to the grant of the current tenancy in order to carry out various improvements to adapt the premises for his use as tenant. The opposite conclusion would be close to an unconscionable attempt by a landlord to take advantage of a situation which it had itself encouraged by consenting to its tenants going into possession and commencing the shopfitting works in advance of the lease.

Scottish & Newcastle Breweries plc v Sir Richard Sutton's Settled Estates (1985)

The rent review clause required a disregard of 'any effect on rent of any improvement or additional building carried out by the tenant or any person deriving title under it'. Before the grant of the lease the landlord was constructing the demised premises. The prospective tenant required some alterations which were carried out by way of a variation to the landlord's building contract, the cost of which was met by the tenant. At the time the parties had entered an agreement for lease.

It was held that the work was carried out by the plaintiff as tenant. Following the approach in the *Hambros* case, the question was whether the improvements were referable to the grant of a tenancy under consideration, or were they referable to some former interest of the tenant, as in the *Wonderland* case? Here they were done in anticipation of the grant of a lease and the occupation by the plaintiffs for the first time of these premises.

4.4.4 What works can be disregarded?

Works can be disregarded if they are carried out to the demised premises and render the tenant's occupation more convenient and comfortable to the tenant.

F W Woolworth & Co Ltd v Lambert (1937)

The plaintiffs held a lease of a shop from the defendants for an unexpired term of 42 years. The lease contained a covenant by the plaintiffs not to erect or suffer to be erected or made on the demised premises any structural alterations or additions, without the previous consent in writing of the lessors. The plaintiffs proposed to enlarge the shop by pulling down the wall at the back and connecting it with other adjoining land of which they held a lease from another lessor, and by erecting over the whole combined property one large shop, in which the main staircase, staff accommodation, etc. would be removed from the demised premises to the extension. The question arose whether the works amounted to improvements within the meaning of the *Landlord and Tenant Act* 1927.

It was held that the works were improvements. It is necessary to consider whether the works are improvements from the point of view of the tenant. The court can only consider improvements of the demised premises themselves. The question is this: 'Will these alterations render the tenants' occupation of the demised premises more convenient and comfortable to them?'

Scottish & Newcastle Breweries plc v Sir Richard Sutton's Settled Estates (1985)

The facts are set out in section 4.4.3.

It was held that the work was not to be disregarded because it was not an improvement to the building provided by the landlord. It was an improvement to the design.

4.4.5 When are works 'carried out' by the tenant?

Improvements are carried out by the tenant if they are carried out by him or if he arranges for a third party to do them. A recital in a deed or licence that the tenant has carried out certain works estops (or precludes) the landlord from contending otherwise.

Scottish & Newcastle Breweries plc v Sir Richard Sutton's Settled Estates (1985)

The facts are set out in section 4.4.3.

It was held that the work was carried out by the plaintiff. They ordered it and paid for it, even though it was actually carried out by the landlords' contractors with the landlords' approval.

Durley House Ltd v Cadogan (2000)

The rent review provisions stated that the rent was to be reviewed to 5% of the freehold value of the property as at the relevant review date on certain assumptions and 'disregarding those matters set out in paras (a), (b) and (c) of section 34 of the *Landlord and Tenant Act* 1954 as amended by the *Law of Property Act* 1969'. The demised premises were serviced apartments. The tenant entered a management agreement with a management company under which it was required to carry out certain works. The question which arose was whether the work carried out by the management company was 'carried out' by the tenant.

It was held that the work was carried out by the tenant.

> 'The tenant will, at least normally, satisfy the statutory requirement if he can establish that he either physically effected the works himself, or got a third party to do so. The tenant will usually satisfy that test if he can show that he had entered into an arrangement with a third party, which arrangement will typically be, but need not necessarily be, a contract, under which that party agreed with the tenant to do the specific works involved in effecting the improvements.'

It was not necessary for the tenant to pay for the work. It would normally be necessary for the tenant to establish some involvement in identifying, supervising and or financing the works.

Daejan Investments Ltd v Cornwall Coast Country Club (1985)

The rent review clause contained a disregard for improvements carried out by the tenant. The parties entered a deed containing an acknowledgement that the tenant had carried out the alterations in a manner satisfactory to the lessor. At rent review, the lessor sought to adduce evidence that the tenant had not in fact carried out the work.

It was held that the lessor was estopped from denying that the tenant had carried out the work. It could, however, seek to set aside the deed on the ground of misrepresentation.

4.4.6 Improvements carried out without consent

The tenant cannot rely on the disregard for improvements for which consent is required unless he has obtained such consent, or the landlord is estopped (or barred) from denying that he has given consent.

Hamish Cathie Travel England Ltd v Insight International Tours Ltd (1986)

The review clause provided that the rental value should be determined on the supposition (if not a fact) that the tenant had complied with all the obligations imposed by the tenancy; and that no account should be taken of the effect of improvements (to which the landlord had given written consent) carried out by the tenant otherwise than in pursuance of an obligation to the landlord. The tenant covenanted not to make alterations without the prior written consent of the landlord. The tenant asked for consent to certain alterations, and the landlord indicated that it approved in principle. No written consent was given. The landlords argued that all improvements should be rentalised. The tenants claimed that consent had been unreasonably withheld and argued:

(1) that it was necessary to imply a term that improvements to which the landlords had unreasonably refused consent should be disregarded;
(2) that in view of the unreasonable refusal the plaintiffs would be taking advantage of their own wrong if the improvements were taken into account;
(3) that, as the review clause required it to be supposed that the tenants had complied with all their obligations, it

must be assumed that they had not carried out the improvements without consent; and

(4) that the landlords were estopped from denying that the tenants had obtained such consent, on the ground of proprietary estoppel or estoppel by convention.

It was held that account should be taken of all the improvements in determining the rental value. As to the tenant's arguments:

(1) it was not necessary to imply a term that improvements to which the landlords had unreasonably refused consent should be disregarded;
(2) the landlord had not unreasonably withheld consent, but even if it had, it had committed no wrong;
(3) it was not to be assumed that the tenant had obtained consent given the express terms of the disregard; and
(4) on the facts, the landlord was not estopped from denying that it had given consent.

4.4.7 Improvements carried out pursuant to an obligation to the landlord

It matters not whether the work is carried out pursuant to a statutory obligation as well as an obligation in the lease.

Forte & Co Ltd v General Accident Life Assurance Ltd (1986)

The rent was to be reviewed disregarding 'the factors set out in subsections (a), (b) and (c) of section 34 of the *Landlord and Tenant Act* 1954'. By the lease the tenant covenanted to carry out all works required to comply with statutory requirements. The tenant carried out works of improvements required to obtain a fire certificate. The tenant argued that the work should be disregarded because it had a choice whether to use the premises for a purpose which required a fire certificate.

It was held that the works were carried out pursuant to an obligation in the lease to comply with statutory requirements, and accordingly they should not be disregarded.

The disregard for improvements is not disapplied merely because the tenant gives covenants as to the manner of carrying out the works in a licence for alterations.

Ridley v Taylor (1965)

The tenant held premises which contained a covenant not to carry out alterations without consent. The tenant wanted to convert the demised premises into flats, and was granted licence to do so. In the licence, which was made under seal the tenant covenanted:

> 'The lessee hereby further covenants with the landlord as follows: (I) ... (II) To complete in a proper and workmanlike manner and with suitable materials to the satisfaction of the estate surveyor of the landlord and in accordance with the said drawing the alterations to the said premises and the works consequent thereon and (III) To do all things necessary and make all payments required for complying with the legal requirements of and obtaining the consent of the district surveyor or any other requisite consent or permission ... of any appropriate public or local authority to the said alterations and works.'

The tenant applied to the Lands Tribunal to modify the covenants, including the covenant in the licence which was assumed to amount to an obligation on the tenant to carry out the works of alteration.

It was held that the covenant to complete the conversion 'to the satisfaction of the estate surveyor' was not a covenant to carry it out, but a covenant that if it was carried out it would be done in a particular manner. If the conversion was not carried out, the lessee remained bound by the original restriction in the lease to use the premises as a single private dwelling house.

Godbold v Martin the Newsagents Ltd (1983)

The rent review clause required there to be disregarded:

> 'Any effect on rent of any improvement of the demised premises or any part thereof carried out by the Tenant

> at the Tenant's expense otherwise than in pursuance of any obligation to the Landlord and carried out during the current tenancy or in respect of which the conditions as contained in section 34 of the *Landlord and Tenant Act* 1954 as amended by section 1 of the *Law of Property Act* 1969 are satisfied.'

The tenant carried out works of improvement pursuant to a licence for alterations which included a number of covenants by the tenant, upon two of which the landlord relied:

> '(a) to carry out the said works of alteration in a proper and workmanlike manner using the best obtainable materials and to comply with the provisions of all Acts of Parliament … and to make good any damage to the demised premises or any part thereof as a result of the works of alteration aforesaid:'

> '(c) to do all things necessary and make all payments necessary for obtaining the consent so far as requisite of any statutory or local authority or owners of adjoining properties and obtain any necessary licence for commencing the aforesaid works of alteration and at his own cost and expense to make good all damage caused through the carrying out of the said works.'

The landlord argued that the improvements should not be disregarded because they were carried out pursuant to the obligations to the landlord in the licence.

It was held that the licence granted permission to the tenant to carry out the work, and did not impose an obligation on the tenant to do so.

4.4.8 How to give effect to the disregard

Valuers should have regard to the intention of the parties in giving effect to the disregard of improvements.

GREA Real Property Investments Ltd v Williams (1979)

The rent review clause included a disregard for improvements. The building was demised as an empty shell. The tenant carried out the necessary works to complete the building. There were no comparables for the shell building. The parties sought guidance on the appropriate method for valuing the demised premises to give effect to the disregard for improvements.

It was held that the valuers should have regard to the imputed intention of the parties, which were as follows:

(1) in view of the possibility of inflation the rent must be reviewed in order to do justice between landlord and tenant;
(2) in view of the tenant's expenditure he was to be credited with the rental equivalent of the works the subject of that expenditure which might itself be affected by inflation; but this was to be the sole benefit which the tenant was to derive from his expenditure (apart from the initial rent-free period which could be disregarded at the review dates);
(3) the improvements themselves would be paid for once and for all at the start of the lease, and at the end of the lease (or any extension) enure for the benefit of the landlord, and in consequence the improvements so far as the tenant was concerned should be regarded as a wasting asset;
(4) the passage of time would mean that at the reviews the improvements would be no longer new; it would be 7- and 14-year-old improvements which fell to be valued;
(5) the valuers in making comparisons of any kind would be careful to compare like with like, bearing particularly in mind that the influence of inflation might differently affect values and costs.

Estates Projects Ltd v Greenwich London Borough (1979)

The lease was granted in 1972 for 53 years, with a rent review every 5 years. On review, there was a requirement to disregard 'any effect on rent of all work carried out by the council in fitting out the demised premises suitable for use as offices and (if applicable) those matters set out in paragraphs (a), (b) and (c) of subsection (1) of section 34 of the *Landlord and Tenant Act* 1954'.

The first floor was improved to allow it to be used for offices, the only permitted use. An arbitrator was appointed to determine the rent in 1977. He took a figure for the cost of improvements and increase it for inflation to 1977 prices. He spread the cost over the whole term, not just the remaining term, and assumed that a sinking fund was provided.

It was held that there was an error of law in the arbitrator's award. To adopt any capital revaluation method to arrive at a rental value in those circumstances was probably not in accordance with the intentions of the parties in at least two respects. Firstly, it is the value of the tenant's works, in rental terms, which has to be eliminated and cost is not necessarily an index of value, though, of course, it may sometimes be so. Secondly, there is involved the assumption that the cost of the improvements will be incurred by the tenant at each review date, whereas the intention of the parties was that the improvements, being already done, the landlord should not benefit from their rental value during the whole of the lease although, of course, the value of them would fall into his pocket, as it were, at the determination of the lease. This also precludes, in these cases, the assumption of a sinking fund.

Where there were comparable premises in an unimproved state, the best approach was to use such comparables.

The right method was probably to calculate the discount for improvements at the time of the demise by comparing the value of the premises as improved with the rent agreed as representing the assessment by the parties of what was in truth the value of the premises, disregarding the effect on rent of the tenant's improvements. The proportion so found could then be applied in the agreed improved rent at the review date, subject to considering the past and future likely effect of inflation on site values, major construction works and works of improvement such as the tenant's, these being the three components which make up the total value of the building.

4.5 FIXTURES AND FITTINGS

The tenant is assumed to have removed chattels and tenants fixtures in the absence of express words to the contrary.

New Zealand Government Property Corporation v HM&S Ltd (1980)

The tenant occupied Her Majesty's Theatre, Haymarket, under a long lease which expired in 1970. The tenant had installed various fixtures and fittings including seats in the auditorium. Following the expiry of the contractual term the tenant remained in possession and the lease continued under the *Landlord and Tenant Act* 1954. The parties negotiated a new lease which was granted in 1973, and contained provision for reviewing the rent after seven years. An issue arose at the first rent review as to whether the premises were to be valued with the fixtures.

It was held by the Court of Appeal that at common law a tenant, other than an agricultural tenant, had a right to remove tenant's fixtures from demised premises so long as he was in possession as a tenant. It was also held that when an existing lease expires or is surrendered and is followed immediately by another, to the same tenant remaining in possession, the tenant does not lose his right to remove tenant's fixtures. He is entitled to remove them at the end of his new tenancy. The open market rental of the demised premises was to be determined on the assumption that the tenant had removed all tenant's fixtures.

4.6 FITTING OUT WORKS

A requirement to assume that the premises are fit for occupation and use normally only precludes a tenant from seeking a discount for the cost of fitting out, and does not require the premises to be valued as fitted out where fitting out works are improvements which fall to be disregarded.

Orchid Lodge (UK) Ltd v Extel Computing Ltd (1991)

The demised premises were let for use only as warehousing. Subsequently an assignee of the lease and the landlord entered a licence to permit alterations to convert the premises to office use. The parties also entered a licence permitting a change of use to offices, subject to a proviso that the rent would be reviewed:

> ' ... on the basis of the authorised use at the relevant review date (the Assignee hereby acknowledging that the Demised Premises are fit for use and occupation therefore) ... disregarding any improvements carried out to the Demised premises by the Tenant ... '.

The assignee duly converted and fitted out the premises for use as offices. The question arose whether the rent review was to be conducted on the assumption that the premises were (a) in their original condition or (b) as altered or (c) in a condition which was reasonable to allow the hypothetical lessee to carry on the authorised (office) use.

It was held that:

- (i) the premises had to be valued in their original condition because of the requirement to disregard improvements; and
- (ii) the acknowledgement that the premises were fit for use and occupation prevented the tenant from claiming a discount on the basis that work had to be done to make the premises fit for the authorised use.

Iceland Frozen Foods plc v Starlight Investments Ltd (1992)

The rent review clause provided for determination of the 'Open Market Rent' defined as

> 'the best yearly rack rent at which the Premises might reasonably be expected to be let as a whole or in parts ... assuming if not the fact that the Premises remain in existence and are ready for immediate occupation and use'

and disregarding improvements.

It was held that the requirement to assume that the premises were ready for immediate occupation and use merely amplified 'remain in existence' and did not require it to be assumed that works of conversion had been carried out.

London & Leeds Estates Ltd v Paribas Ltd (1993)

In this case the assumption in question was:

> 'That the demised premises are fit for immediate occupation and use and in a state of good repair and

condition and that all fitting out and other tenant's works required by such willing tenant have already been completed.'

The case was initially argued before the Court of Appeal on the basis that the arbitrator on a rent review had to determine what fitting out and other works would have to be carried out. The court rejected this approach. Nourse LJ, in a judgment with which Stuart-Smith and Waite LJJ agreed, said at p150H:

> 'The clear purpose of the first part of clause 6(b)(1) is to preclude the *actual* tenant from arguing before the arbitrator that the *hypothetical* tenant would be entitled to a discount on the best open market rent on account of the *actual* state of repair and condition of the premises. It is impossible to read that provision as having any other purpose or effect. Equally, the purpose of the second part of clause 6(b)(1) must be to preclude the actual tenant from arguing for a discount on the ground that the hypothetical tenant would have required further or different works from those carried out by the actual tenant, the cost of which would necessarily be borne by the hypothetical tenant, with a corresponding reduction in the rent that he would be willing to pay. There is simply no warrant for reading into the second part of clause 6(b)(1), any more than into the first part, some requirement for the arbitrator to determine what hypothetical works the hypothetical tenant would have required. If the parties had intended that there should be such a requirement, they could and should have made express provision for it.'

Ocean Accident & Guarantee Corporation v Next plc; Commercial Union Assurance Co plc v Next plc (1996)

The rent was to be reviewed:

> 'Assuming:
>
> (B) that the Demised Premises have been fully fitted out and equipped so as to be ready for immediate use and occupation by such willing tenant for such a use
>
> (C) that all the Tenant's obligations herein have been

complied with

(E) that any additions or alterations carried out on or to the Demised Premises during the Term which have diminished the rental value of the Demised Premises have been removed or reinstated

but Disregarding:

(H) any increase in rental value of the Demised Premises attributable to the existence at the Relevant Review Date of any improvement to the Demised Premises …'.

By clause 3(27) of the lease, the tenant covenanted:

'(a) Immediately upon the grant of this lease (if and to the extent that such works shall not prior thereto have been so carried out) to equip and fit out each part of the Demised Premises for the purpose for which the Demised Premises may be used as permitted hereunder and for such ancillary purposes thereto as may be appropriate for each such part.

(b) Throughout the Term to ensure that each part of the Demised Premises remains fully equipped and fitted out as aforesaid in accordance with the standards appropriate to a good class shop.'

The 'demised premises' were defined as 'the property described in the Schedule hereto and all additions and improvements from time to time made thereto and the landlord's fixtures and fittings therein'.

The arbitrator had determined that the tenant's fixtures should be rentalised. It was held that this was an error of law, and that tenants' fixtures should not be rentalised.

It was held by the deputy judge that the function of assumption (B) was simply to avoid an argument that the hypothetical tenant requires an allowance in reduction of his rent on the basis that the premises are not immediately ready for him to trade.

The definition of 'demised premises' did not include tenant's fixtures, because they were not 'additions' or 'improvements' (see the *New Zealand Government Property Corporation* case in section 4.5), and because of the express reference to the landlord's fixtures and fittings.

Assumption (C) required the arbitrator to assume that the tenant had equipped and fitted out the premises in accordance with clause 3(27)(a), and ensured that the premises remain fully equipped and fitted out in accordance with clause 3(27)(b). It was, however, inappropriate to require the arbitrator to rentalise tenant's fixtures or chattels which the tenant was entitled to remove at the end of the term.

4.7 ASSUMED TO BE LET AS A WHOLE

The property is assumed to be let as a whole, not in parts, unless express provision is made.

Marklands Ltd v Virgin Retail Ltd (2004)

The reviewed rent was to be calculated on the basis of 'a letting of a store'. The landlord argued that in hypothetical negotiations, a willing lessor could threaten to divide up a large unit unless the tenant were willing to pay a sufficiently high and acceptable rent in order to secure a lease of the whole.

It was held that it was not permissible to have regard to the possibility that the lessor might enter a different transaction.

Iceland Frozen Foods plc v Starlight Investments Ltd (1992)

The rent review clause provided for determination of the 'Open Market Rent' defined as:

> 'the best yearly rack rent at which the Premises might reasonably be expected to be let as a whole or in parts … assuming if not the fact that the Premises remain in existence and are ready for immediate occupation and use'

and disregarding improvements.

It was argued by the landlord:

- that the premises could be divided and let separately in seven self-contained units;
- that it should be assumed that such units had been converted into self-contained accommodation because of

the assumption that they were ready for immediate accommodation and use, and

- that the necessary works should not be disregarded because they were only hypothetical improvements, not improvements actually carried out.

It was held that:

- the assessment of the new rent was to be on the basis of the rental value of the premises in their actual condition for the time being, not on the basis that the hypothetical landlord or tenant will have carried out works of conversion necessary to subdivide the premises into seven units;
- since rent should not be charged for actual improvements, the rent could not be reviewed on the basis that the tenant should be charged for hypothetical improvements which had not been carried out;
- the requirement to assume that the premises were ready for immediate occupation and use merely amplified 'remain in existence' and did not require it to be assumed that works of conversion had been carried out.

Lewisham Investment Partnership Ltd v Morgan (1997)

The claimant alleged that the expert who determined the rent review was negligent in failing to have regard to the ability of the tenant to divide the unit up into three or four smaller units.

The lease was of a large unit in Lewisham shopping centre with a frontage of 145ft onto the central mall. The lease permitted underleases of not more than three separate parts. There was a qualified covenant against alterations. The rent review clause provided for determination of 'the rent at which the demised premises might ... reasonably be expected to be let as a shell building' on the same terms as the lease, disregarding the tenant's occupation, goodwill and tenant's improvements.

The expert considered himself bound by the decision in *Iceland* to disregard the possibility that the premises could be subdivided.

It was held that the expert was not negligent, but that the judge (Neuberger J) would not have followed the decision in

Iceland, which he considered wrong for the following reasons:

> 'It seems to me, with respect, that this reasoning confuses rentalising improvements with rentalising the right to carry out improvements. Improvements are physical things which, under the terms of the instant rent review clause and that in *Iceland*, must not be rentalised; the right to carry out improvements is wholly different. The logic of the decision would seem to lead to surprising conclusions. For instance, it would appear to follow that one should disregard the hypothetical tenant's rights to occupy, and to build up goodwill in, the premises, because the actual tenant's occupation and goodwill must, under the terms of the rent review clause, be disregarded. Also, as Mr Reynolds pointed out, it would appear that where, as here, the premises to be valued are a 'shell' one could not take into account the possibility (which in practice would be a certainty) that the hypothetical tenant would effect *immediate* and substantial improvements to the premises.'

Neuberger J also considered the decision in *Iceland* to be contrary to the presumption of reality, because the 'reality' was that the premises were not divided but that the tenant had the right at any time during the lease to carry out works of alteration to subdivide the premises into a number of different units, and then to sublet those units.

Westside Nominees v Bolton MDC (2001)

The rent payable under the lease of a six-storey office building was to be reviewed to the 'best rent at which the premises might reasonably be expected to be let in the open market by a willing lessor whether as a whole or in parts whichever is the greater'. At the time of the demise, it was anticipated that the defendant would occupy the whole building apart from the ground floor which would be sublet in two parts. This subletting was specifically permitted by the lease. There was a qualified covenant against subletting, and an absolute covenant against alterations, the effect of which was to prevent alterations which would be required for further subdivision of the building. An issue arose as to the assumptions which could be made about division of the building if it were valued in parts. The tenant contended that it was to be treated as divided only as specifically permitted by the lease, or as actually divided up.

It was held that in valuing the building in parts, the valuer should assume 'a reasonable organisation of the demised premises', subject to the constraints on subdivision flowing from the covenant against alterations. It was not unfair that the tenant should pay the aggregate value of the separate parts, rather than receiving a discount which a tenant of the whole would require. That pass had been sold by agreeing to the possibility of valuing the building in parts.

4.8 RIGHTS OF ACCESS ATTRIBUTED TO THE PROPERTY OR HYPOTHETICAL TENANT

Where the property is landlocked it is questionable whether any rights of access should be implied.

Jefferies v O'Neill (1984)

Solicitors who owned the freehold of their own premises took a lease of upper floors of adjoining premises for additional office accommodation. The only access to the demised premises was at first-floor level through the solicitors' own freehold premises, the staircase in the demised premises having been removed. The tenants argued on review that the demised premises should be valued on the basis that they could not be let to anyone else. The rent review clause, however, provided for the rent to be that at which the demised premises might reasonably be expected to be let on the open market by a willing lessor to a willing lessee. It was held, applying the principle of *Law Land Company Ltd v Consumers' Association Ltd* (1980), that the reviewed rent should be determined on the basis of an implied disregard of the fact that access to the demised upper-floor accommodation was only through the lessees' own adjoining premises and not independently from ground-floor level.

British Airways plc v Heathrow Airport Ltd (1992)

British Airways held a lease of a number of different plots of land at Heathrow Airport. The rent was to be reviewed to:

> 'The total of the current annual market rental values of those plots comprising the Second Premises if let individually on a building lease for a term of years equivalent in length to the term of years hereby granted such lease being on the same terms and conditions (other than as to amount of rent but including the provisions as to review of rent and excluding the First Premises and the provisions of this lease solely relating to the First Premises) as this present demise without the payment of any fine or premium.'

Certain plots did not enjoy independent rights of access, and the court was asked to determine whether on the hypothetical letting of any such plot, the valuer was to disregard the lack of such access when determining the current market rental value of each such plot.

It was held that a disregard of the lack of access should be implied to give commercial efficacy to the rent review clause because without it, it was it was difficult to see here how there could be a market for a hypothetical lease of the property.

J Murphy & Sons Ltd v Railtrack plc (2002)

The tenant held a lease of property to which access could only be gained over adjoining freehold property owned by the tenant. The tenant applied for a new tenancy under Part II of the *Landlord and Tenant Act* 1954. The landlord contended that there should be an implied statutory disregard of the lack of access in determining the new rent.

It was held that there was no justification for implying such a disregard. Peter Gibson LJ questioned the correctness of *Jefferies v O'Neill* and *British Airways v Heathrow Airport* on the ground that in neither case had consideration been given to the principle established by the *Indian* case, that the existence of a special purchaser was an appreciatory factor, since he would make more than a nominal bid to reflect his interest in acquiring the property.

5
The hypothetical lease

5.1 THE BASIC PROVISION

Rent review clauses normally require a determination of what would be payable by a willing tenant to a willing lessor on a hypothetical letting in the open market. Reference to a 'reasonable', 'fair' or 'full market' rent for the premises does not alter the basis of the determination.

Ponsford v HMS Aerosols Ltd (1979)

The rent review clause provided for the rent to be the higher of the passing rent or 'a reasonable rent for the demised premises'. There was no express disregard for improvements. The tenant made extensive improvements with the consent of the landlord, and contended that they should be disregarded because of the reference to a 'reasonable' rent.

It was held by the majority of the House of Lords that the task of the expert was not to assess what would be a reasonable rent for the lessees to pay but what is a reasonable rent for the premises in the open market, regardless of who provided the improvements or paid for them. The use of the word 'reasonable' would enable the expert to disregard someone who would be prepared to offer an exceptionally high rent or freak rent.

If the lease had provided for determination of 'such rent … as the court in all the circumstances thinks reasonable' or 'which it would be reasonable for the tenants to pay' the surveyor would have been entitled and bound to have regard to the particular circumstances of the tenant.

99 Bishopsgate Ltd v Prudential Assurance Co Ltd (1985)

The rent review clause provided for the rent to be 'amount which shall in [the arbitrator's] opinion represent a fair yearly rent for the demised premises ... having regard to rental values'.

It was held that 'fair' meant not fair between the particular parties to the lease, but what a hypothetical tenant would fairly be expected to pay if taking the premises from a hypothetical landlord.

ARC Ltd v Schofield (1990)

The rent review clause provided for the rent to be 'a fair and reasonable market rent'.

It was held that this required determination of a market rent, not having regard to the circumstances of the actual parties to the lease.

Royal Exchange Assurance v Bryant Properties (Coventry) Ltd (1985)

The rent review clause in a lease of a warehousing estate comprising 32 units provided for payment of either the passing rent or 75% of the 'full current market rack rental value of the demised premises'. It was argued by the landlord that the arbitrator had to determine the rent on the basis of the aggregate rental values of the individual units without applying any discount which an investor taking a lease of the whole estate would require because of the word 'full'. It was held that the word 'full' did not add to or change the requirement to determine the market rent.

5.2 IN THE ABSENCE OF A FORMULA OR BASIS FOR DETERMINATION

In the absence of any formula or basis for determination, the rent must be fixed by reference to what the particular parties would have agreed.

Thomas Bates and Son Ltd v Wyndham's (Lingerie) Ltd (1981)

The lease as rectified provided for the rent to be reviewed to 'such rents as shall have been agreed between the lessor and the lessee or shall in default of such agreement be determined by a single arbitrator.'

It was held that, in default of agreement between the parties, the arbitrator would have to assess what rent it would have been reasonable for these landlords and these tenants to have agreed under this lease, having regard to all the circumstances relevant to any negotiations between them of a new rent from the review date.

5.3 WILLING LESSOR AND LESSEE

The hypothesis of an open market letting requires it to be assumed that there would be a willing lessor and a willing lessee.

Dennis & Robinson Ltd v Kiossos Establishment (1987)

The rent was to be reviewed to the open market rent, but there was no reference to a willing landlord or tenant. It was argued that no tenant would take the premises. It was held that the requirement to assume an open market letting meant that it had to be assumed that:

(1) there would be a letting of the property;
(2) there is a market in which that letting is agreed; and
(3) the landlord is willing to let the premises.

Equally, the supposed tenant is willing to take the premises. The notion of a letting in the open market between an unwilling lessor and an unwilling lessee (or between a willing lessor and an unwilling lessee) for the purpose of determining a reasonable rent makes no sense.

The willing lessor and lessee do not possess attributes of the actual lessor and lessee which would not be possessed by any willing lessor or lessee.

Evans v English Electric Co Ltd (1978)

The lease contained a rent review clause which provided that the rent should be the rent at which the premises were worth to be let on the open market, as between willing lessor and willing lessee, but disregarding the matters there set out, which are in substance the matters set out in paras (a) to (c) of section 34(1). The arbitrator made findings that:

(1) There was no other property on the market that provided the accommodation and facilities provided by the subject property.
(4) Apart from the present tenants, it was very unlikely on the available evidence and on the state of the market that there would have been a potential tenant in the market for the subject premises on the terms of the lease offered.
(5) In October 1976, if the present tenants had not been in occupation of the subject premises, they would not have made any bid for the lease being offered.
(6) The present tenants in October 1976 could have split their operation into parts and could have moved each of those parts into smaller alternative premises in the United Kingdom.

The court was asked to give guidance on what assumptions should be made about the willing lessor and lessee, and the extent to which they possessed the characteristics of the actual landlord and tenant.

It was held that the rent had to be determined in the light of all circumstances which in fact affect the property and in theory affect the hypothetical lessor and lessee. Any circumstance which affects the actual landlord and actual tenant, but which would not affect the hypothetical landlord and tenant is irrelevant.

In a well known and much quoted judgment, approved by the Court of Appeal, the judge described the hypothetical negotiations as follows:

> 'the negotiations were to be assumed to be friendly and fair but otherwise conducted in the light of all the bargaining advantages and disadvantages existing on that date;
>
> that for the purposes of the clause the willing lessor was not the plaintiff landlords but a hypothetical person with the right to dispose of the premises on an 18-year lease, not afflicted by personal ills such as a cash-flow crisis or importunate mortgagees nor being

someone to whom it was largely a matter of indifference whether he let … or waited for the market to improve but wanting to let the premises at a rent which was appropriate to all the factors which affected the marketability of the premises … including the market rent of competitive premises, i.e. premises which were directly comparable or would be considered as viable alternatives … ;

that, similarly, the willing lessee was a hypothetical person, not being, nor necessarily having any of the characteristics of the defendant tenants, actively seeking premises to fulfil needs which the demised premises could fulfil, taking account of similar factors to those taken into account by the willing lessor but similarly unaffected by liquidity problems, governmental or other pressures to boost or maintain employment in the area and so on;

that the rent was to be agreed in the light of all the circumstances which in fact affected the demised premises and in theory affected the hypothetical lessor and lessee, but that any circumstance which affected the plaintiff landlords or the defendant tenants but which would not affect the hypothetical lessor and lessee was irrelevant;

that the fact that there was no other property on the market which provided the accommodation and facilities provided by the demised premises was relevant, but that the hypothetical tenant, being neither reluctant nor importunate, would take account of the alternative of taking a lease of two or more other premises;

that the fact that it was very likely that the defendant tenants would have been the only potential lessees of the premises was only indirectly relevant, since a single potential lessee was nevertheless to be assumed to be a willing lessee and to remain a willing lessee so long as the willing lessor did not press his demand for rent beyond the point at which he was ceasing to act as a willing lessor and at which a willing lessee would cease to be such.'

Railtrack plc v Guinness Ltd (2003)

The respondent developer required an access road over railway lines owned by Railtrack plc and London Underground. During negotiations Railtrack plc offered to sell access rights for £9.7 million. The parties could not agree on the consideration and agreed to refer the dispute to the Lands Tribunal on the basis that it was to determine 'the open market value of the rights required for access over the Railway'. The Tribunal determined the consideration at £5 million, having regard, among other things, to the offer made by Railtrack plc. Railtrack plc appealed on the ground that the Tribunal failed to assume a sale by a willing seller, but instead assumed a sale by a company regulated and subsidised by central government and subject to the same political pressures as Railtrack plc.

It was held that it had to be assumed that there was a willing seller, who was a hypothetical seller, but the Tribunal was not required to ignore the fact that the seller was necessarily a railway company. It was therefore entitled to have regard to the offer made by Railtrack plc in negotiations as evidence of what a willing seller would offer.

A special purchaser is not to be disregarded.

IRC v Clay (1914)

The open market value of a house had to be determined on the footing that it had been sold on the valuation date in the open market by a willing seller. It was only worth £750 for residential purposes, but it adjoined a nursing home, the trustees of which desired to extend their premises and they would have paid £1000. The case for the Crown was that the special needs of the trustees had to be disregarded or alternatively that it should be assumed that the trustees needed only marginally more than £750 to secure the property.

It was held that the neighbouring owner was part of the open market, and their bid was not to be disregarded. It was also wrong to assume that the special purchaser would only have to make one more bid above what other bidders were willing to pay. The value was held to be £1000.

Vyricherla Narayana Gajapatiraju v Revenue Divisional Officer, Vizagapatam ('The Indian Case') (1939)

Land was compulsorily acquired by harbour authorities because it contained a spring yielding good drinking water which could be made available to oil companies and people engaged in harbour works and which had the particular attraction to the acquiring authority that water could be used to supply the local population whose wells, a source of malaria-carrying mosquitoes, could then be closed. The fact that malaria was endemic in the area might otherwise have made the development of the harbour uneconomic. Lord Romer stated the principle applicable in cases of compulsory acquisition in a well-known passage:

> 'The compensation must be determined, therefore, by reference to the price which a willing vendor might reasonably expect to obtain from a willing purchaser. The disinclination of the vendor to part with his land and the urgent necessity of the purchaser to buy must alike be disregarded. Neither must be considered as acting under compulsion. This is implied in the common saying that the value of the land is not to be estimated at its value to the purchaser. But this does not mean that the fact that some particular purchaser might desire the land more than others is to be disregarded. The wish of a particular purchaser, though not his compulsion, may always be taken into consideration for what it is worth.'

The value of the land must be determined having regard to the potential uses of it and the potential profit to be made from it by a special purchaser. The valuer must ascertain the price that would be paid by a willing purchaser with its potentiality.

First Leisure Trading Ltd v Dorita Properties Ltd (1991)

The tenant held separate leases of the main part of the Greyhound Hotel, Croydon, and the ground floor reception area ('the extension'). The lease of the extension contained a restriction on use save as an extension to the hotel, and a rent review clause. The reversions to the two leases were severed, and a dispute arose as to the assumptions to be made in reviewing the rent for the extension. The two questions for determination were:

Question 4: Whether the arbitrator could find that the plaintiff was a possible hypothetical tenant.

Question 5: Was the arbitrator required to assume that the possible hypothetical tenants bidding in the open market were restricted to those persons who were prepared to take the risk of seeking and obtaining the consent of the owner and occupier of the immediately adjoining premises, formerly known as the Greyhound Hotel, to use the demised premises as an extension to those said adjoining premises?

It was held, after reviewing *Evans v English Electric*, *Cornwall Coast Country Club v Cardgrange*, *IRC v Clay* and the *Indian case*, that there was no principle of law which required the arbitrator, while having regard to the fact that First Leisure was the lessee of the Greyhound, to assume that First Leisure was not a potential lessee of the extension. First Leisure could not be identified as the hypothetical lessee; adopting Donaldson J's words, 'His profile may or may not fit that of First Leisure'. But in ascertaining the best rent that would be obtainable in the open market, the arbitrator had to take into account the potential value of the extension to a lessee of the Greyhound Hotel.

Accordingly, the answer to question 4 was that strictly the arbitrator was not required to assume either that First Leisure was or that it was not a possible hypothetical tenant. But he was entitled to find as a fact that a lessee of the Greyhound Hotel, whoever he might be, would be a potential tenant. It was for him to say what effect that fact, if found, would have as between a hypothetical willing lessor and a hypothetical willing lessee negotiating the terms of a hypothetical lease of the extension.

It followed that the answer to question 5 was 'no'.

Daejan Investments Ltd v Cornwall Coast Country Club (1985)

The demised premises were occupied by a subtenant who carried on a casino business for which it held a gaming licence. The rent review clause required there to be disregarded any gaming licence held by the tenant.

It was held that there was no reason to disregard the subtenant as a potential bidder.

The willing lessor is willing to enter the transaction in question. The rent should not be determined by reference to some other transaction.

Northern Electric plc v Addison (1997)

The tenant held a lease of an electricity substation, and applied for a new tenancy under the 1954 Act. The parties agreed the terms of the new lease, including a restriction on use to that of a substation. The landlord and his expert contended that the market rent was £1000 per annum because if the tenant had to go elsewhere it would have to incur the expense of moving and pay a rent which reflected other potential uses of the land. The tenant's expert considered the rental value to be £15 per annum, based on comparable evidence of other substation leases.

The judge was required to assume a willing lessor of premises limited to use as an electricity substation, the term already agreed between the parties.

It was held that this combination of considerations necessarily precluded a notional lessor unwilling to let the premises for such restricted use, unless a premium was paid to take into account other potential uses. That was because:

(a) such an approach would represent a qualification on the overall notion of a willing lessor whose willingness falls to be judged on the assumption that it relates to the lease before the court;

(b) taking into account other potential uses involves ignoring what are in fact terms providing for one use and one use only.

Marklands Ltd v Virgin Retail Ltd (2004)

The reviewed rent was to be calculated on the basis of 'a letting of a store'. The landlord argued that in hypothetical negotiations, a willing lessor could threaten to divide up a large unit unless the tenant were willing to pay a sufficiently high and acceptable rent in order to secure a lease of the whole.

It was held that it was not permissible for the landlord to say that he could enter into a different kind of transaction, when he was known to be willing to enter into that which the lease prescribes.

5.4 VACANT POSSESSION AND SUBLETTINGS

In the absence of a specific assumption of vacant possession, it depends on the facts of each case whether the hypothetical letting is with vacant possession, or subject to sublettings existing at the review date. Relevant considerations are whether it was contemplated when the lease was granted that the demised premises would be sublet at the date of review, whether the initial rent was related to the rents receivable from subtenants, and the terms of the review provisions.

Avon County Council v Alliance Property Co Ltd (1981)

The plaintiff granted a lease for 125 years pursuant to an agreement for lease which contemplated that the lease would be subject to underleases granted for 25 to 35 years with the approval of the tenant. The initial rent was fixed by reference to the cost of developing the premises, not by reference to the rent receivable from underlessees. The rent was to be reviewed to 70% of the rack-rental market value of the demised premises. The question arose whether the rent was to be reviewed on the assumption of a letting with vacant possession or subject to the existing underleases.

It was held the words 'with vacant possession' were implicit. A rack-rent is the best rent that can be reasonably obtained and the best rent would ordinarily be obtained in respect of premises in vacant possession. Furthermore, the initial rent under the lease was not intended to be fixed by any reference to the scheduled leases.

Scottish & Newcastle Breweries plc v Sir Richard Sutton's Settled Estates (1985)

Judge Baker accepted the submission that vacant possession valuation is likely to be the intention unless it is expressed to the contrary. He added that 'Were it otherwise the landlord would be in the position of a review of rent of being in the hands of the tenant if the tenant decides what terms he is to arrange with the subtenant'.

It was held in this case, however, that there should not be an assumption of vacant possession. The two main factors were firstly that the subletting of all the other floors and the part of the ground floor was contemplated and agreed to from the outset, and, indeed, the original rent was calculated by reference to the rents receivable from subletting, and the formula then adopted found its place for certain purposes in the current review provision. Secondly, the sublettings were themselves subject to review at the same date as the review under the head lease.

Forte & Co Ltd v General Accident Life Assurance Ltd (1986)

The premises were demised in 1967 for a term of 35 years subject to an underlease of part for a term of 54 years from 1949 under which the rent was fixed at £3,000 per annum. The rent payable under the head lease was subject to five-yearly reviews, with no direction as to whether the letting was with vacant possession. The issue was whether the hypothetical letting was with vacant possession or subject to the underlease.

It was held by Peter Gibson J that it would be very surprising if the parties had intended that the rent review would proceed on the footing, contrary to reality, that the property subject to the 1949 underlease was available for letting with vacant possession so the value of that part could exceed £3,000. Although the ascertainment of an open market rental of premises which were let with vacant possession would ordinarily involve an assumption of vacant possession, different considerations applied when part of the premises were already subject to a tenancy in favour of a third party, the term of which would continue beyond the review date. It was not a necessary part of the hypothesis of an open market letting that such a tenancy should be ignored, and reality should not be departed from more than was necessary to give effect to the assumptions required by the rent review clause.

Hill Samuel Life Assurance Ltd v Preston (1990)

A 99-year building lease was granted on terms which contemplated that the different units in the building would be sublet. The rent was to be reviewed to 'the market rack rental value at the date of review', there being disregarded, among other things:

> 'The fact that the Lessees or their predecessors in title or any persons claiming under or through them **are** or have been in occupation of the premises'.

It was held that the direction to disregard occupation at the date of the review made it clear that the hypothetical letting was with vacant possession.

Laura Investment Co v Havering London Borough Council (1993)

On 14 June 1972 the Greater London Council granted the defendants a lease for 62 years of about five acres of undeveloped land. There were 15-year rent reviews which required the rent to be assessed on the assumption that the premises were a bare site. The rent review clause did not say that the hypothetical letting was to be with vacant possession. It simply required determination of 'the market rental value' at the rent review date. The only expressed assumption was that all covenants and conditions in the lease have been duly observed and performed.

One of the covenants required the tenant:

> 'as speedily as possible, subject to the provisions of subclauses 3(h), 3(n) and 3(s) hereof, to underlet the demised premises in separate plots and to cause to be erected on each of such plots factory or warehousing premises together with associated premises.'

The lease also contained a covenant not to underlet without written consent, not to be unreasonably withheld, and specific consent to the grant of a building lease of one plot for the whole 62-year term, less a few days.

It was held that the rent was to be calculated on an assumption of reality, that is to say, assuming the existing underlettings to be in place.

If there were a presumption of vacant possession, it conflicted with the presumption of reality. Even if there were a presumption of vacant possession, it was somewhat weakened if the terms of the lease protect the landlord against being made subject to the arbitrary acts of the tenant in the terms on which he underlets.

In this case,

- the terms of the lease, including the fact that underlettings were contemplated, indeed mandated, by the terms of the lease,
- the fact that the landlord could reasonably refuse consent to underlettings, and
- the terms of the rent review clause,

pointed to the conclusion that the parties intended the rent to be calculated on an assumption of reality, that is to say, assuming the existing underlettings to be in place.

It was not possible to draw a hard and fast line between cases such as *Forte* in which there is an existing underletting at the time of the grant, and cases in which the underletting is contemplated or even agreed, but not yet actually completed.

5.5 HEADLINE RENT

Where the rent is determined on the assumption of a letting with vacant possession, the rent is likely to be discounted because a tenant would need time to fit out and/or sublet the premises. Rent-free periods are granted to reflect the time and cost of fit out, and also to inflate the 'headline rent'. 'Headline rent' clauses are to be construed as preventing any discount for the fit out element of the rent-free period, but not as preventing adjustment of comparables to reflect the second element in the absence of very clear words.

99 Bishopsgate Ltd v Prudential Assurance Co Ltd (1985)

The rent review clause provided that the amount to be determined by the arbitrator was that which in his opinion represented a fair yearly rent for the demised premises at the valuation date, having regard to rental values then current for property let without a premium with vacant possession.

The demised premises comprised 300,000 sq ft of offices at 99 Bishopsgate. They were so large that any hypothetical tenant would only occupy part, and would sublet the rest. The arbitrator found that if he were required to value the building with vacant possession, a tenant would require an 18-month period of rent-free occupation in order to find subtenants and allow the latter a rent-free period to fit up the premises. This resulted in a substantial reduction in the rent spread over the term, from £6,700,000 to £6,065,000. The issue was whether the premises should be valued with vacant possession.

It was held that they should.

Co-operative Wholesale Society Ltd v National Westminster Bank plc, Broadgate Square plc v Lehman Brothers Ltd, Scottish Amicable Life Assurance Society v Middleton Potts & Co and Prudential Nominees Ltd v Greenham Trading Ltd (1995)

The Court of Appeal heard four appeals together concerning the correct construction of headline rent clauses. Hoffman LJ gave the following general guidance:

> ' ... in the case of rent-free periods, it is easy to see why the parties should not wish to allow the tenant a reduction simply because the fiction of vacant possession entails that the incoming tenant would have the expense of moving in and fitting out. A clause which excludes the assumption that he would have this expense is more in accordance with the presumption of reality than one which does not. On the other hand, a clause which deems the market rent to be the headline rent obtainable after a rent-free period granted simply to disguise the fall in the rental value of the property is not in accordance with the basic purpose of a rent review clause. It enables a landlord to obtain an increase in rent without any rise in property values or fall in the value of money, but simply by reason of changes in the way the market is choosing to structure the financial packaging of the deal.

> It therefore seems to me that, in the absence of unambiguous language, a court should not be ready to construe a rent review clause as having this effect. On the other hand, it would not be right to treat it as simply preposterous.'

The court first set out the general principles, as summarised above, and then applied them to the wording of the lease in each of the appeals. The decisions on the particular provisions were as follows.

Co-operative Wholesale Society Ltd v National Westminster Bank plc

The lease was dated 8 August 1986 and the relevant words are as follows:

> 'The rental value in the open market of the demised premises at the relevant date of review for a term … commencing on the relevant date of review in the open market as between a willing lessor and a willing lessee with vacant possession on the supposition … that any rent-free period or concessionary rent or any other inducement whether of a capital or revenue nature which may be offered in the case of a new letting in the open market at the relevant date of review shall have expired or been given immediately before the relevant date of review.'

It was held that the headline rent derived from the comparables must be discounted to allow for any rent-free period not attributable to the fact that the hypothetical tenant has still to enter into occupation of the premises.

The assumption that the rent-free period was past necessarily implied that the tenant must be treated as already having moved in. The tenant could not, therefore, argue for the equivalent of a rent-free period for fitting out. But it did not mean that, by reason of the previous rent-free period, the tenant had committed himself to the new term. He must be treated as free if necessary to move out, instantly and without cost, if he can obtain comparable premises elsewhere for less. This construction gave the clause the effect of negativing the *99 Bishopsgate* fitting-out allowance, but no more.

Broadgate Square plc v Lehman Brothers Ltd

The lease was dated 31 December 1987 and the relevant words are as follows:

> ' "Open Market Rent" means the best yearly rent which would reasonably be expected to become payable in respect of the premises after the expiry of a rent-free period of such length as would be negotiated in the open market, between a willing landlord and a willing tenant upon a letting of the premises as a whole by a willing lessor to a willing lessee in the open market at the relevant Review Date for a term of ten years or a term equal to the residue of the then unexpired period of the Term (which ever is the longer) with vacant possession without fine or premium.'

It was held that these words left no escape from the conclusion that the open market rent is to be the headline rent. Unlike the previous case, the rent-free period was not deemed to have expired before the parties negotiate. The rent to be applied to the whole term was the rent which would become payable after the expiry of such rent-free period as would be negotiated on the review date, i.e. the headline rent. The reference to the rent-free period being of 'such length as would be negotiated in the open market' made it impossible to confine the words to rent-free periods attributable to the tenant having to move in.

Scottish Amicable Life Assurance Society v Middleton Potts & Co

The lease was dated 25 September 1987 and the relevant words were as follows:

> 'The New Rent shall be the greater of (a) the Existing Rent (b) such sum as shall be agreed by the Lessor and the Lessee or determined as representing the best yearly open market rent (at the rate payable following the expiry of any rent-free period or periods at concessionary rents which might be granted on a new letting of the Demised Premises or of comparable premises on the relevant review date) at which the demised premises might reasonably be expected to be let in the open market on the relevant Review Date

> without a fine or premium or value in the nature of a fine or premium …
>
> But disregarding:
>
> (d) any effect on rent of any initial rent-free period or periods at concessionary rents or other inducements which might be offered in the open market to prospective underlessees of the Demised Premises or any part thereof or of comparable premises.'

It was held that this clause merely prevented a tenant from claiming a fitting-out discount.

Unlike *Broadgate Square* the clause did not simply refer to whatever rent-free period would be negotiated between a willing lessor and willing lessee in the open market. It specified the rent-free period which 'might be granted on a new letting of the demised premises or of comparable premises'. Arden J was correct to hold that a new letting meant a letting to a new tenant who needed to move in rather than, for example, a renewed letting to a tenant who is already there. The rent-free period to which the clause referred was one which was attributable to the letting being new. It did not, therefore, include a rent-free period granted to induce the tenant to pay a higher rent than he would otherwise have done, since this would be just as much a characteristic of a renewed letting to a tenant in occupation as of a letting to a new one.

This construction was reinforced by the emphasis on the lease being granted 'without a fine or premium or value in the nature of a fine or premium'. A rent-free period to secure a higher headline rent was in the nature of a (reverse) premium, whereas a rent-free period which is genuinely for moving in and fitting out would not be described as in the nature of a reverse premium.

Prudential Nominees Ltd v Greenham Trading Ltd

The lease was dated 1 March 1988 and the relevant words were:

> 'the best at which the whole of the premises might reasonably be expected to be let in the open market on the relevant review date by a willing landlord to a

> willing tenant with vacant possession and without taking any fine or premium ... upon the assumptions that ...
>
> (4) no reduction or allowance is to be made on account of any rent-free period or other rent concession which in a new letting might be granted to an incoming tenant.'

It was held that this clause merely prevented a tenant from claiming a reduction for fitting out.

The arbitrator was required in the first part of the clause to determine the rent which a tenant in the open market would pay over the whole of the hypothetical term. Assumption (4) provided that no reduction was to be made or allowance given from such rent because a tenant in the real market might be given a rent-free period. There was no warrant in the clause for increasing this figure from the market rent to a headline rent because tenants in the market were being given rent-free periods.

St Martin's Property Investments Ltd v CIB Properties Ltd (1999)

The rent was to be reviewed:

> 'On the assumption that the said willing tenant or tenants do not seek a rent-free period nor any reduction in rent to allow them the equivalent of a rent-free period and in considering any comparable rents the existence of any rent-free period or any reduction in rent calculated to allow for any rent-free period shall be ignored'.

It was held that the clause should be construed as directing the valuer to arrive at a market rent on the assumption that there would be no rent-free period for start up and no reduction would be sought. Comparables could be used, but rent-free periods and reductions for start-up periods had to be ignored and striped out. That was supported by the presumption of reality. The landlord's claim for a headline rent, which would be in excess of the market rent, would not accord with the presumption of reality.

5.6 THE NOTIONAL TERM

In accordance with the presumption of reality, the hypothetical letting would be for the same term of years and from the same commencement date as the actual lease in the absence of clear contrary words or necessary implication.

Norwich Union Life Insurance Society v Trustee Savings Banks Central Board (1986)

The rent review clause in a lease granted for a term of 22 years from 29 September 1972 provided that the new rent was to be assessed on the assumption that the premises were being let in the open market 'on the terms and conditions of this lease'.

Hoffman J interpreted this hypothetical lease as running for 22 years from 29 September 1972, rather than from the rent review date and commented:

> 'There is, I think, a presumption that the hypothesis upon which the rent should be fixed upon a review should bear as close a resemblance to reality as possible. In this case the reality was that at the date of the rent review the tenant's interest was an unexpired period of 10 years ... The purpose of the rent review is to enable that rent to be adjusted at a subsequent date in order to take into account the effects of inflation and changes in the market since the original grant. I think that the landlord would be having it both ways if he was entitled not only to an adjustment for changes in the market and changes in inflation but also the assumption that what was being granted on the rent review date was a brand new lease rather than what was in fact the case, a lease which by then was 12 years expired.'

Ritz Hotel (London) Ltd v Ritz Casino Ltd (1989)

In a lease granted for 21 years from 1 July 1977, the rent review clause provided for a comparison with similar properties let on similar terms 'for a term equivalent to the term hereby granted'. The landlords contended that this provision required an assumption that the premises were let for a term of 21 years from the review date. The tenants submitted that the hypothetical term was 21 years from 1 July 1977.

Adopting the approach in *Norwich Union v TSB*, Vinelott J held for the tenants. The landlords' interpretation overlooked the reality that time had passed since the grant of the lease and could easily lead to a 'manifestly unjust result'. One such example would be a lease for 21 years with five-yearly reviews and an onerous repairing covenant of a building specially constructed for a particular purpose and with a limited life intended to be coterminous with the expected demand for that use.

In any event, the 'natural construction' of the 'term equivalent to there term hereby granted' was a term of 21 years from 1 July 1977, of which 10 years had expired at the date of the review.

Lynnthorpe Enterprises Ltd v Smith (Sidney) (Chelsea) Ltd (1990)

The underlease in question was for 15 years from 22 August 1978. There was a fixed rent for the first 9 months, followed by a higher fixed rent for the next 9 months. For the subsequent 18 months, the rent was to be that payable immediately prior to the commencement of this third period, or the fair market rent at that time, whichever was the higher. Further rent reviews followed at three-yearly intervals.

The rent review clause provided that the hypothetical tenancy should be 'a tenancy for the term of years equivalent to the said term', the 'said term' being the term granted by the underlease.

The Court of Appeal interpreted this provision as requiring a hypothetical term of 15 years from 22 August 1978, rather than from the date of review. Dillon LJ, with whom Taylor and Stanton LJJ agreed, held that this followed from the general principle that, if the language used in a rent review clause permits, the clause will be interpreted as requiring the notional letting to be a letting on the same terms (other than as to quantum of rent) as those still subsisting between the parties in the actual existing lease: for a term of 15 years from the review date would give the tenant a longer term than he actually has.

Moreover, a hypothetical term of 15 years from the review date would 'run into difficulties, when compared with reality', since the assessment for the first three-year period, which contained fixed rents for the first 9 months and a review after 18 months, was different to that for the subsequent three-year periods with which the case was concerned.

Tea Trade Properties Ltd v CIN Properties Ltd (1990)

The rent review clause for a lease of 24 years from 24 June 1970 provided that the hypothetical tenancy be 'for a term of years and on conditions and terms similar to the terms hereof'. Hoffman J held that this meant a tenancy for a term of 24 years from 24 June 1970 and commented:

> 'There are a number of cases in which the courts have decided that, unless the language of the lease shows clearly that some artificial assumption was to be made, it should be presumed that the hypothetical letting should, as closely as possible, reflect what the landlord at that date actually has to offer.'

Hoffman J saw nothing in the language of the rent review clause in that compelled him to conclude that the artificial assumption should be made of a tenancy for a term of 24 years from the date of review. The provision was indistinguishable from that in *Lynnthorpe*.

St Martin's Property Investments Ltd v CIB Properties Ltd (1999)

The underlease in question was for a term of 35 years commencing on 24 June 1986. The rent review clause provided that the hypothetical tenancy was to be 'for a term equal in duration to the original term hereby granted' and that it was to be 'otherwise upon the terms and conditions of this Underlease' save as to rent.

Aldous LJ, with whom Arden and Buxton LJJ agreed, held that this amounted to a term of 35 years commencing on

24 June 1986 rather than on the date of the review, for three reasons.

Firstly, the 'duration of the original term' granted by the underlease was 35 years from a specific date, namely 24 June 1986.

Secondly, an assumption of a lease of 35 years from the review date in 1996 could not be 'upon the terms and conditions' of the actual underlease, since it would be inconsistent with the terms providing for specific rent review and determination dates.

Thirdly, the Court's conclusion was consistent with the purpose of a rent review clause, which was 'to enable the landlord to obtain from time to time the market rental which the premises would command if let on the same terms on the open market' and which therefore required an assessment that reflected the true position.

Canary Wharf Investments (Three) v Telegraph Group Ltd (2003)

The underlease in question was for a term of 25 years from 1 April 1992. The rent review clause in question defined 'open market rent' as the rent at which the premises, subject to certain assumptions:

> ' ... could be expected to be let as a whole at the Relevant Review Date by a willing landlord to a willing tenant with vacant possession and without payment of receipt by any person of any consideration, under the rent, for the grant thereof, for a term of 25 years ... '

The landlords contended that the 'term of 25 years' ran from 1 April 1992; the tenants that it ran from the review date.

Neuberger J held for the tenants. The presumption of reality was not a mechanistic rule of construction, to be applied rigidly in every case. The rent review clause in *Norwich Union* contained no specific reference to the hypothetical term, and so the presumption was the only factor upon which the court could fall back to decide on the hypothetical term. In *Ritz* and *St Martins*, the natural meaning of the words used in the rent review clause was held to be in accordance with the presumption and, therefore, there was strictly no need to invoke the presumption. The same could be said of the clause at issue in *Lynnthorpe*, where the rent review frequency also militated against a longer hypothetical term.

Accordingly, the presumption of reality could not override the natural meaning of the rent review clause. The natural meaning of 'for a term of 25 years' in this case was that the hypothetical lease ran from the review date. This view was particularly reinforced by the words 'for the grant thereof': there was no such thing as a retrospective grant, so the landlord's interpretation would amount to a grant for a term of only 15 years.

Chancebutton Ltd v Compass Services UK & Ireland Ltd (2004)

The lease, dated on 23 June 1989, was for a term of 25 years (less one day) from 24 June 1982. It was subject to a five-year rent review to the market rate, which was to be assessed on the assumption that the premises were let 'for a term equal to the term originally granted'. The landlords contended that this hypothetical term was for 25 years (less one day) commencing on 24 June 1982. The tenants contended that it was for 25 years (less one day) from the date of the rent review.

Reviewing the case law, Lawrence Collins J commented that the trend was towards the presumption of reality: this meant that 'in the absence of clear contrary words or necessary implication, it is assumed that the hypothetical letting required by the clause is of the premises as they actually were, on the terms of the actual lease and in the circumstances as they actually existed'. The presumption was not a mechanistic rule, but an example of how the commercial approach to construction was the starting point.

The Court held in favour of the landlords. It was irrelevant that the lease did not take effect as a grant until 23 June 1989, seven years after the date on which it was expressed to commence and also after the date for first payment of rent and the first review date. It was very common for leases to take effect from a prior date, and it would be anomalous if similar wording that was common in rent review clauses bore different meanings depending upon whether the lease was granted before or after the tenant took possession.

The natural meaning of the expression 'for a term equal to the term originally granted under this lease' was a term sharing not only the duration of the actual lease but also its date of commencement. Had the parties intended the assumption at each review to be 25 years from the review date, it would have been easy for them to have said so. The tenant's construction required a departure from reality which was, therefore, unjustified by the language of the rent review clause.

5.7 RIGHTS UNDER THE *LANDLORD AND TENANT ACT* 1954

Regard may be had to the value of rights under the *Landlord and Tenant Act* 1954 (LTA 1954) in the absence of a provision to the contrary.

Pivot Properties Ltd v Secretary of State for the Environment (1980)

The rent review clause in a business lease defined 'rack rental market value' as 'the best rent at which the demised premises might reasonably be expected to be let in the open market ... for a term not exceeding five years and one half of another year'.

The question referred to the court by the arbitrator was whether any 'account is to be taken of any possibility of the tenancy being continued or renewed under the provisions of the *Landlord and Tenant Act* 1954'.

The Court of Appeal noted that the LTA 1954 did not 'continue or renew' tenancies, save in limited circumstances; it provided for the grant of new tenancies. Accordingly:

> 'to take account of the possibilities under the Act of 1954 was not to assess the rent for a term longer than five and a half years but to assess it for a term of five and a half years one of the potentialities of which was that it might be continued or renewed'.

Both parties must have envisaged that at the review dates they would have to retain the services of professional valuers who would be likely to apply such methods as were from time to time commonly accepted by valuers. At the date of review, these methods included taking into account the effect on the rents of business premises of the rights given to tenants under LTA 1954. Accordingly, this effect was a relevant consideration in the valuing the 'rack rental market value' for the purposes of the review.

Toyota (GB) Ltd v Legal & General Assurance (Pensions Management) Ltd (1989)

The rent review clause in the first lease defined 'open market value' by reference to a hypothetical lease for 'a term of years certain equivalent in length to the residue unexpired at the review date of the term of years hereby granted'. The clause also provided that there should be disregarded 'all restrictions relating to security of tenure contained in any statute'.

In relation to a review on 25 March 1988, the tenant contended that the hypothetical lease would be with no security of tenure under Part II of the *Landlord and Tenant Act* 1954.

The Court of Appeal held that the words used in the rent review clause did exclude from consideration the provisions of Part II of the LTA 1954.

5.8 BREAK CLAUSES

A personal break clause should not be incorporated into the hypothetical lease.

St Martin's Property Investments Ltd v CIB Properties Ltd (1999)

In a lease with a personal break clause in favour of the tenants, the hypothetical tenancy for the purposes of rent review was to be 'upon the terms and conditions of this Underlease'. The Court of Appeal held that this did not grant a personal right to the hypothetical tenant to break the lease. The words of the actual lease could only be modified for the purposes of the hypothetical lease if it would otherwise be impossible to have an open market letting. That was not the case in relation to a personal break clause, which in a hypothetical lease would simply be otiose (serve no practical purpose).

5.9 RENT REVIEWS UNDER HYPOTHETICAL LEASE

A requirement to assume a hypothetical letting on the same terms as the actual lease containing words such as 'other than the rent hereby reserved' is generally construed as requiring the amount of the rent, but not the rent review clause or other provisions relating to rent, to be disregarded.

British Gas Corporation v Universities Superannuation Scheme Ltd (1986)

The rent payable on review under a 35-year lease with five-yearly reviews was to be the rack rental value at which the demised premises could reasonably be expected to be let in the open market for a term equal to the term granted by means of a lease 'containing the same provisions (other than as to the yearly rent)' as the actual lease.

There were three possible constructions of the words in brackets:

(1) that they required the valuer to ignore all provisions relating to rent in the lease;
(2) that they required the valuer to ignore those provisions which relate to the quantification of rent, i.e. the rent payable immediately before the relevant review date and the provisions for future rent reviews;
(3) that they required the valuer to ignore the rent actually payable before the review date only, i.e. he must take into account the provisions for future reviews of the rent.

It was held that the valuer was only required to ignore the rent actually payable before the review date. The judge gave the following general guidance on the construction of similar provisions.

'The correct approach is as follows:

(a) words in a rent exclusion provision which require all provisions as to rent to be disregarded produce a result so manifestly contrary to commercial common sense that they cannot be given literal effect;

(b) other clear words which require the rent review provision (as opposed to all provisions as to rent) to be disregarded (such as those in the *Pugh* case,) must be given effect to, however wayward the result;

(c) subject to (b), in the absence of special circumstances it is proper to give effect to the underlying commercial purpose of a rent review clause and to construe the words so as to give effect to that purpose by requiring future rent reviews to be taken into account in fixing the open market rental under the hypothetical letting.'

Equity & Law Assurance Society plc v Bodfield Ltd (1987)

The premises were demised for 70 years with rent reviews every 14 years. The reviewed rent was to be 85% of net rental value.

Clause 4(2) provided that in determining the rent it was to be assumed that the premises were let 'upon the terms of this lease other than as to duration and rent'.

The Court of Appeal approved the guidelines stated in *British Gas Corporation v Universities Superannuation Scheme* (set out above).

It was held that the rent review provisions could not be incorporated into the hypothetical lease because they provided for calculating 85% of the net rental value. Where the lease provides for payment of rent at a discount or premium to market value, that term must be excluded from the terms of the hypothetical lease unless expressly provided to the contrary.

In cases providing for a geared rent, or payment of an additional rent, the rent is normally to be reviewed assuming a lease without the gearing or additional rent provisions, in the absence of clear words.

Guys 'n' Dolls Ltd v Sade Brothers Catering Ltd (1984)

Paragraph 1 of the rent review clause provided that after the first review date the rent of the premises should be £7,500 above the fair rack rental market value, which was to be:

> 'for a term of years equivalent to the then unexpired residue of the term hereby granted ... and in all other respects on the terms and conditions of this lease'.

Paragraph 2 stated that there was to be a similar £7,500 additional rent in respect of the second review date.

The Court of Appeal held that the words 'in all other respects on the terms and conditions of this lease' meant 'in all other respects on the terms of this lease, in addition to the provision relating to the duration of the term which has already been referred to'. Literally, this was wide enough to include the obligation to pay additional rent.

It was clear, however, that the intention of the parties was that the annual rent should be maintained at £7,500 above the market rental value of the premises. If the additional rent was not disregarded, the market value would be reduced and produce a result which would frustrate this intention. Accordingly, the rent review clause was interpreted as requiring the rent to be determined on the assumption of a letting without the additional rent.

Buffalo Enterprises Inc v Golden Wonder Ltd (1991)

The rent payable under the lease comprised of a basic rent, which was fixed for the first five years and subject thereafter to review, and an 'additional rent', which was 15% of a capital sum of £60,000 which had been spent by the landlord on the premises. It was further provided that this 15% was to be increased pro rata with the increase in the basic yearly rent. The review formula for the basic rent provided for an assessment of:

> 'the fair yearly market rental of the premises as it shall then be let on the terms and conditions (except as to yearly rent) herein stipulated for the residue of the said term of years'.

The tenant contended that the hypothetical lease should be assumed to include the obligation to pay additional rent.

Hoffman J held that, on this view, the assessment would have a circularity which the parties are highly unlikely to have intended: namely, that the market value would take into account the additional rent, which would itself depend on the market value.

Moreover, the tenants' construction would mean that at the first review date the additional rent would in practice disappear, since the market value would be reduced by the amount of the initial rent. As in *Guys 'n' Dolls*, this was hardly likely to have been the parties' intention.

Accordingly, the proper construction was to disregard the additional rent altogether for the purpose of reviewing the basic rent.

Prudential Assurance Co Ltd v 99 Bishopsgate Ltd (1992)

According to the provisions of this lease, the rent payable following review was to be whichever was the greater of the rent payable during the last relevant year or 50.6% of the 'yearly rental value' of the premises as at the appropriate date. The 'yearly rental value' was to be assessed by reference to a hypothetical tenancy having regard 'to the provisions of the actual lease (other than the rent hereby reserved)'.

Mummery J held that the natural meaning of the words in brackets was to exclude from the hypothetical lease the amount of rent which the tenant had to pay under the actual lease. On such a construction, the reference to the fixed percentage of 50.6% should be excluded from the hypothetical lease, since it was merely a term as to the quantum of rent.

The fixed percentage had no more relevance to the valuation of the actual lease than those provisions of the actual lease which specify a fixed sum of additional rent to be payable over and above the market rent, such as that in *Guys 'n' Dolls*.

British Railways Board v Ringbest Ltd (1996)

Following the five-year rent reviews, the rent payable was whichever was the higher of the rent payable during the previous period or 84.0253% of the 'market rent'. The market rent was defined by reference to a hypothetical lease 'subject to provisions similar to those contained in this Subunderlease (including rent reviews)'.

The arbitrator had decided that the provision for 'similar' rent review provisions in the hypothetical lease required a rent review clause in the same terms as in the actual lease. Accordingly, the determined market rent was higher than it might otherwise have been to reflect the advantage of the 16% reduction. The tenants' application for leave to appeal was refused. Sir Richard Scott VC acknowledged that the arbitrator's interpretation largely negated the benefit of the tenant's reduction, but held that the language of the clause, and in particular the words 'including rent reviews' made it very difficult to reach any other construction.

Norwich Union Life Assurance Society v British Telecommunications plc (1995)

A 'gearing provision' in the rent review clause provided that the rent payable following each review was the previous rent increased by the proportion to which the market rent of comparable office accommodation in Birmingham exceeded 100p per sq ft. The notional letting of the comparable accommodation was to be assessed on the assumption that the 'landlord and the tenant undertook the respective obligations which they have undertaken in this underlease'.

The landlord contended that the parties could not have intended the gearing provision itself to be imported into the notional letting of comparable accommodation, since if that affected the value of the comparable the entire object of the exercise would be defeated.

Knox J held for the tenant. The words 'provided that the landlord and tenant undertook their respective obligations which they have undertaken in this underlease' were clearly words of inclusion rather than exclusion. In excluding the gearing provision the court would be rewriting, not interpreting, the parties' agreement. While there was an element of illogicality in importing the initial principal rent which covered both office and back premises in the mathematical formula, this did not produce anything like the self-cancelling absurdity in *Guys 'n' Dolls*.

The arbitrator has no power to determine a stepped rent, or a rent subject to further review.

National Westminster Bank Ltd v BSC Footwear Ltd (1981)

A lease for 21 years contained an option for the tenant to renew for a further term of 21 years 'at the then prevailing market rent', to be determined by arbitration in default of agreement, the new lease to be subject in all other respects to the same covenants, provisos and conditions as the original lease. The question arose whether the arbitrator had power either to determine a rent which was subject to periodic review, or to fix a differential or progressive rent.

It was held that the arbitrator had no power to introduce a provision for periodic review or determine a differential or progressive rent. The option clause referred to the prevailing rent, not to the prevailing use and practice of the market at the date of renewal. The arbitrator had to determine a single rent payable throughout the term of the new lease.

Scottish & Newcastle Breweries plc v Sir Richard Sutton's Settled Estates (1985)

The lease was for a term of 42 years. The rent was to be reviewed once, after 21 years, by:

> 'ascertaining the annual rack rent of the demised premises including any buildings thereon at the date of the rent notice that is to say the annual rent at which the demised premises and any such buildings might reasonably be expected to be let as a whole without premium in the open market as between a willing landlord and a willing tenant *if the tenant undertook to pay all usual tenant's rates and taxes and to bear the cost of repairs, insurance and other expenses (if any) necessary to maintain the same in a state to command such rent ...'*

No other provision was made for the length or terms of the hypothetical letting.

The tenant contended that terms of the lease should be the terms specified (in italics) and those which the property is most likely to be let at in the open market at the due date, including some provision for review, since no one would let for 21 years without some review date.

It was held that the arbitrator should review the rent on the basis that it was to be on the terms of the existing lease other than as to rent for the period of 21 years.

The expression of some terms in the review provision did not leave the rest of the provisions at large to be incorporated or not as the arbitrator might decide. The choices open were either no terms at all other than those indicated in the review provision, or those in the existing lease in so far as they were not inconsistent with the express terms in the review provision. In fact they were not inconsistent with the terms in the lease.

5.10 USE

Where there is absolute covenant against use other than a specific use, the rent must be determined without taking account of the possibility that the landlord would agree to a change of use. The position is different where the lease contemplates changes of use.

Plinth Property Investments Ltd v Mott Hay & Anderson (1977)

The tenant covenanted not to use premises otherwise than 'as offices in connection with the lessee's business of consulting civil engineers'. There was no provision for change of use with the landlord's consent. The rent review clause of the lease required the rental value to be fixed having regard to the provisions of the lease. The arbitrator fixed the rental value on the footing that the rent was to be assessed in accordance with the provisions of the lease including the user covenant allowing the one use only.

It was held that the arbitrator was right to value the rent on the terms of the lease including the provision that only one use was permitted. He was not entitled to take into account the possibility that the landlord might consent to a change of use.

Forte & Co Ltd v General Accident Life Assurance Ltd (1986)

The case concerned a rent review under several leases with detailed user provisions which contemplated changes of use with the consent of the lessor and superior lessor. The question arose whether the arbitrator could take into account the possibility of a change of use.

It was held that the decision in *Plinth Property* does not apply to a case where the lease expressly contemplates that other forms of use might be authorised. It would be open to the arbitrator to say that the possibility of the superior lessors acting arbitrarily, as they were entitled to do, when asked for their authority had the effect in valuation terms that the rental value had to be assessed on the footing that the specified forms of use are the only permitted forms of use. But equally, the arbitrator was entitled to say that the hypothetical lessee would pay more for a lease which expressly contemplated the possibility of a change of use.

Where the user clause restricts use to the business of the named tenant, the rent review should normally be conducted on the basis that the hypothetical lease restricts use to the business of the hypothetical tenant to give effect to the commercial purpose of the review clause.

Law Land Company Ltd v Consumers' Association Ltd (1980)

The rent was to be reviewed to the rent at which the demised premises might be let in the open market with vacant possession by a willing lessor and subject to the provisions of the lease. The tenant covenanted 'not, without the prior written consent of the landlord, to use or permit the demised premises or any part thereof to be used, other than as offices of the Consumers' Association and its associated organisations'.

It was held that there would be no market rent or open market if the premises could not be used by the hypothetical lessee, and there would be no point in offering vacant possession to the hypothetical lessee if the premises could only be occupied and used by the Consumers' Association and its associated organisations before and after the grant of the hypothetical lease to the hypothetical lessee. Accordingly when it comes to a rent review the revision is in respect of a hypothetical lease in which the original hypothetical lessee will be subject to a covenant whereby the premises can only be used as offices for the purposes of that hypothetical lessee and its associated organisations, if any.

Sterling Land Office Developments Ltd v Lloyds Bank Ltd (1984)

Lloyds Bank held a lease of premises for a term of 42 years subject to review after 21 years. The tenant covenanted not to use the premises 'for any purposes other than as a branch of Lloyds Bank'. The rent was to be reviewed to 'an amount equal to the market rental for the demised premises with vacant possession'. The issue which arose was what terms as to use were contained in the hypothetical lease.

It was held, following *Law Land*, that the covenant in the hypothetical lease would read 'That the demised premises shall not be used for any purposes other than as premises of the hypothetical willing lessee'.

James v British Crafts Centre (1986)

The term granted by the lease was one of 14 years from 29 September 1976. The rent originally reserved by the lease was £10,500 per year.

The tenant covenanted:

> 'not to use or permit or suffer the demised premises or any part thereof to be used for any purpose other than
>
> (i) for high class business commercial or professional offices ... or
>
> (ii) in respect of such part of the demised premises as shall for the time being be occupied and used by the Lessee (here meaning The British Crafts Centre party hereto) for storage sale and display of craftsmen's work and ancillary offices and in respect of the first floor of the demised premises (whilst not occupied and used by

> British Crafts Centre) as an office and studio for the trade or business of designers advertising and press agents.'

The hypothetical lease for the purpose of the rent review was to be on the same terms as the actual lease. The lessor contended that the user covenant left a space for the name of the hypothetical tenant in place of 'The British Crafts Centre'.

It was held that there was no need to change the wording of the covenant in the hypothetical lease. *Law Land* was distinguishable because there was an alternative permitted use of the whole premises as offices. The right to use part for crafts was personal to the current tenant.

The lease may provide for the rent to be reviewed on the assumption of a hypothetical different use from the actual user provisions of the lease. Such a provision will displace the presumption of reality where the words are clear.

Sheerness Steel Co plc v Medway Ports Authority (1992)

The lease contained a covenant by the tenant not to use or occupy the premises other than for the purposes of steel-making, steel-rolling and operations ancillary thereto or for such other purposes as may from time to time be approved by the lessors. The reviewed rent was to be:

> 'the amount which shall represent a fair yearly rent for the Site having regard to the rental values then current for property let for one hundred and twenty five years from the date of valuation, without a premium with vacant possession for industrial purposes ... and otherwise on the terms and conditions of this Lease (other than the rent hereby reserved) ... '.

The question for determination was whether or not the notional lease incorporated the covenant as to use and, if so, what restrictions on use there would be in the notional lease.

It was held that the rent review required an assumption of a letting with the user provision modified so as to permit use for industrial purposes or for such other purposes as might from time to time be approved by the landlord (such approval not to be unreasonably withheld). The word 'otherwise', clearly gave a predominance to the words 'for industrial purposes' over the actual user clause.

The notional lessee was to be regarded as being entitled to carry out all alterations necessary or appropriate to convert the premises for an industrial use of his choice, notwithstanding the covenant in the actual lease by the tenant not to carry out alterations or improvements save in connection with the use of the premises for steel-making.

Postel Properties Ltd v Greenwell (1992)

The permitted use was 'as a retail shop within the meaning of Class I of the *Town and Country Planning (Use Classes) Order* 1972, for the retail trade or business of the retail sale of high quality chinaware and crystal-ware and, as ancillary thereto, high quality enamel-ware and pottery.' The premises were put to this use at the review date. The rent review provision required determination of:

> 'the rent at which, having regard to the terms hereof (other than as to rent but taking an account of these present provisions for a review of rent), the demised premises might reasonably be expected to be let for retail purposes without premium in the open market by a willing lessor to a willing lessee, it being assumed that the demised premises are to be let with vacant possession and in good repair and condition and for a term of the same number of years as the term, but commencing from the commencement of the relevant revision year.'

It was held that the direction to assume a letting for retail purposes displaced the presumption of reality, and the premises were to be valued on the basis of a letting for retail purposes.

Burford UK Properties Ltd v Forte Hotels UK Ltd (2003)

The rent under a lease of a hotel was to be determined by reference to the net bedroom revenue (NBR), defined as:

> 'the gross amount … received in respect of charges for bedroom accommodation at the hotel … provided that the tenant shall at all times use its best endeavours to

> obtain the maximum revenue from the use of bedrooms as sleeping accommodation'.

The question arose whether, if the tenant failed to maximise revenue, the rent was to be determined on the assumption that it had maximised revenue, or whether the landlord had to sue for damages.

It was held that the word 'received' should be read as 'receivable', and the rent review should be conducted on the assumption that the tenant had maximised revenue.

Where the lease directs the assumption of a different use in the hypothetical lease, it must also be assumed that the premises can be used for that purpose lawfully, without any breach of covenant or planning control. It need not however be assumed that the premises have been physically adapted for the specified use unless such works were required to comply with the tenant's covenants in the lease.

Bovis Group Pension Fund Ltd v GC Flooring & Furnishing Ltd (1984)

The rent review clause provided for determination of 'The rent at which having regard to the terms hereof (other than as to rent and user) the demised premises might reasonably be expected to be let for office purposes'. In fact the premises were used as a mixture of showrooms and offices. There was no planning consent for use of the whole as offices, and the tenant contended that regard should be had to the uncertainty a tenant would face over whether planning permission would be granted for office use.

It was held that the rent should be determined on the assumption that the permitted use was for offices, and that it was a lawful use for which planning permission had been granted.

Trust House Forte Albany Hotels Ltd v Daejan Investments Ltd (1980)

Premises at 366–375 Strand, and the Strand Palace Hotel were demised for 75 years from 5 July 1963 at an initial rent of £550,000 per annum subject to review at seven-year periods thereafter. The rent review clause required determination of the market value:

> '... of those areas being parts of the ground floor and the basement of the demised premises as shown edged red on the plans annexed hereto and marked C and D (on the basis that those areas are actually let for or are available for letting for shopping and retail purposes)'.

In fact the premises in question were partly being used as part of the hotel at the review date, and would have required substantial works to convert them to be used for shopping and retail purposes.

The issue was whether the valuation was to be made on the basis of the premises in their actual physical state, or on the basis that such part of the premises as was not let as shops at the review date was to be treated as being in a state reasonably appropriate for such use.

It was held that the clause did require it to be assumed that any necessary planning permission to enable use for shopping or retail purposes had been given, and that any provisions in the underlease which might prevent such use or alteration of the premises for such use had been suitably varied or waived or appropriate consents given. The premises would not be 'available' for a purpose if there were in existence lawful prohibitions, whether statutory or contractual, against the use of the premises for such purpose. But premises could be available for shopping and retail purposes irrespective of their physical condition.

> 'Availability, does no more than assume that the premises are on offer with vacant possession and that they can be used for the specified general purpose without illegality or breach of covenant. The supposed new lessee may or may not need physical alterations of the premises to carry out the shopping or retail use which he contemplates ... '.

The landlord should not get the benefit of assumed alterations which he has not made.

Little Hayes Nursing Home Ltd v Marshall (1983)

In 1985 the defendants granted a lease of a guest home for the elderly for a term of 12 years with an option to acquire the freehold at any time after 19 October 1988. At the time of the grant of the lease the lessors had carried on at the property the business of providing a guest house for the elderly with 25 beds. They were registered under the *Registered Homes Act* 1984 (the '1984' Act). It was a condition of their registration that the total number of persons received into the home should not exceed 25.

The lease contained covenants not to make alterations or additions without the licence of the landlord. It also provided that the use of the property should remain that of a guest house for the elderly, and that the tenant should comply with statutory requirements.

After the grant of the lease the lessees continued the business for a while, but they were unable to continue to satisfy the requirements of the local authority for registration under the 1984 Act and the home was closed.

In 1987 the lease was assigned to the plaintiffs, who wished to reopen the home and gave notice to the defendants exercising the option to acquire the freehold. Subject to completion of certain works the local authority was prepared to allow its reopening as a home with maximum of 17 beds.

A question arose as to the open market value of the property for purposes of the purchase and sale under the option agreement. The option provided that in determining the value, it was to be assumed 'that the user of the Property remains that of a Guest House for the Elderly as at the date hereof and that the sale is with vacant possession'.

Issues arose as to what assumptions should be made as to whether the guest house was actually in use, whether the necessary works had been carried out, and the number of beds to be assumed.

It was held that:

1. It was to be assumed not just that the property could be used as a guest house for the elderly in the same manner as at the date of the lease, but that it was being so used.

2. It therefore had to be assumed that registration under the 1984 Act had been obtained.
3. The assumption that the property was actually in use at the valuation date as a guest house for the elderly in respect of which registration was required and had been obtained made it necessary to assume that any works necessary to enable the property lawfully to be so used had been carried out. Otherwise the tenant would be in breach of its obligation in the lease to comply with statutory requirements. *Trust House Forte Albany Hotels Ltd v Daejan Investments Ltd* (1980) was distinguished because in that case it was not necessary to assume that the property was being used for the assumed use, merely that it could be so used.

5.11 PLANNING CONTROL

No value can be attached to the possibility of use in breach of planning control, but value can be attributed to the possibility of obtaining permission for a particular use.

Compton Estates Ltd v Estates Gazette Ltd (1977)

The lease contained a user clause and a covenant to comply with statutory requirements.

It was held that in determining the reviewed rent the arbitrator should exclude from consideration the possibility of any future use of the premises in breach of planning control.

6th Centre Ltd v Guildville Ltd (1989)

The building was at one time a warehouse. The first and second floors had been used throughout the leases for offices and showrooms. The authorised use of these floors for planning purposes was for warehouse purposes, and the current office use was therefore unauthorised. Planning permission was refused for office use in 1976. In fact no proceedings had been taken against the tenants in respect of the office use, which was continuing. That use was unlawful.

The lease provided that the premises would not be used otherwise than as showrooms or offices. However, recognising that there was no planning permission for such uses, it also provided that, if enforcement proceedings required the termination of office use, the lessees would use their best endeavours to obtain the necessary permission but if after having exhausted all rights of appeal the enforcement notice or any subsequent enforcement shall be effective, then the lessee would discontinue the office use at the demised premises.

It was held that the valuation should be made on the basis that the premises may be used during the hypothetical term only for warehouse purposes in accordance with the planning permission in force as at 1 November 1986 but should have regard also to any prospect that planning permission for use as offices could be obtained during the said term. No doubt in estimating that value, the valuer would note that office use had in fact been going on to the knowledge of the authorities for some time without objection.

The surveyor had to assume that there would be compliance with the covenants and that the use of the building, if used at all, would be lawful. Therefore, it would not be right to value the premises on the assumption that they might lawfully be used as offices or on the basis that the actual, though unlawful, use would continue during the term but with the possibility that the tenant might be forced to abandon it.

Daejan Investments Ltd v Cornwall Coast Country Club (1985)

The demised premises were used as a casino, the most valuable use. The user clause permitted a variety of uses. The rent review clause required the occupation of the tenant and any gaming licence held by the tenant to be disregarded. The landlord argued that it should be assumed that the hypothetical tenant held a gaming licence, since otherwise the permitted use could not lawfully be carried on.

It was held that since there was no direction to assume a particular use, and there were a variety of permitted uses, there was no justification for assuming that the hypothetical tenant held a gaming licence.

6
Procedure for determining the reviewed rent

6.1 INTRODUCTION

Many rent reviews are settled by agreement between the parties without the need for a third party to determine the rent. However, in some cases the parties will be unable to agree. As explained in chapter 3, the rent review clause should provide a procedure for the reviewed rent to be determined if the parties cannot agree. The choice is normally between determination by an arbitrator and determination by an expert. A well-drafted clause will state which method is to be used. It will also provide a method for the appointment of the surveyor if the parties cannot agree. That method will normally be appointment by the President of the RICS. If time is of the essence for the application to the President, then the application must be made within time and in accordance with the procedures laid down by the appointing body: *Staines Warehousing Co Ltd v Montague Executor & Trustee Co Ltd* (1987). Where time is of the essence for the appointment and application is made out of time then, in the absence of agreement by both parties, any decision by the surveyor will not be binding as there will have been no effective appointment: *Darlington Borough Council v Waring & Gillow (Holdings) Ltd* (1988).

6.2 THE DISTINCTION BETWEEN DETERMINATION BY AN ARBITRATOR OR BY AN EXPERT

In some review clauses the method of determination is either not specified, or not clearly specified, with the result that the court must decide in what capacity the third party is to act. General guidance on the distinction between an arbitrator and an expert is available in two cases in the House of Lords, concerning an architect employed under the RIBA contract and a firm of accountants valuing shares. More specific guidance is available in a series of rent review cases.

6.2.1 General guidance on the distinction

It would appear from the cases below that the key question is whether the third party is obliged to exercise a judicial function in making a determination. In other words is he to conduct a judicial inquiry by hearing the parties and the evidence of witnesses and to arrive at a decision upon that evidence or is he entitled to act solely upon his own expert opinion.

Sutcliffe v Thackrah (1974)

An architect appointed under the RIBA form of building contract was held by the House of Lords not to be an arbitrator and was therefore not immune from liability for negligence. An arbitrator was described by the House of Lords as a person appointed by agreement to determine a specific dispute or defined differences that might arise in the future and there was agreement that this decision would be binding.

Arenson v Casson Beckman Rutley & Co (1975)

An accountant appointed to value shares was held to be an expert and not an arbitrator. It was held by the House of Lords that the essential prerequisite for appointment as an arbitrator is that, by the time the matter is submitted to him for decision, there should be a formulated dispute between at least two parties which his decision is required to resolve. It is not enough that parties who may be affected by the decision have opposed interests – still less that the decision is on a matter which is not agreed between them.

6.2.2 Specific guidance in rent review cases

More specific guidance is given in a number of cases concerning rent review clauses. Relevant factors in determining the issue will include a comparison with other dispute resolution provisions in the lease, the use of words referring to arbitration or to the *Arbitration Acts*, whether the valuer is to receive submissions and the nature of the task (determination of a value or resolution of a dispute) given to the third party.

Langham House Developments Ltd v Brompton Securities Ltd (1980)

A lease for 42 years provided for rent reviews in which the rent was to be 'determined by a chartered surveyor nominated by the President [of the RICS]'. It was held that the surveyor was to act as an expert as there was a clear contrast between this clause and an earlier clause providing for certain other disputes to be resolved by a single arbitrator in accordance with the provisions of the *Arbitration Act* 1950.

Safeway Food Stores Ltd v Banderway Ltd (1983)

A lease for 90 years provided for rent reviews in which, in the event of the parties' valuers not having reached agreement, an umpire was to settle the question. It was held that the umpire was to act as an expert because there was a contrast with another clause in the lease providing for reference to a single arbitrator, the whole issue was one of expertise in arriving at a rent and the umpire was to supply the place of a valuer.

Fordgate Bingley Ltd v Argyll Stores Ltd (1994)

A lease for 35 years provided for rent reviews in which, if the parties should not agree, the rent was to be determined by a surveyor whose determination was to be final and binding. It was held that the surveyor was to act as an expert because there was a deliberate non-adoption of any express reference to arbitration, the clause did not presuppose any dispute and the exercise was particularly suitable for expert procedures.

Coventry Motor Mart Ltd v Corner Coventry Ltd (1997)

A rent review clause provided for determination of the rent by 'a single member of the Chartered Surveyors Institute'. It was held that the surveyor was to act as an expert, there being another contrasting clause in the lease dealing with arbitration.

6.3 THE CONSEQUENCES OF THE DISTINCTION BETWEEN AN EXPERT AND AN ARBITRATOR

The consequence of the distinction can be significant. For example, an arbitrator is immune from liability in negligence (section 29(1) of the *Arbitration Act* 1996) whereas an expert may be sued for negligence. Also, there is a limited right of appeal against an arbitrator's award whereas there is no right of appeal against an expert's determination.

The RICS guidance notes for *Surveyors Acting as Arbitrators and as Independent Experts in Commercial Property Rent Reviews* (8th edition) provide a useful comparison of the consequences of the distinction between an expert and an arbitrator as set out in the following table.

Arbitrator	*Independent expert*
a. The arbitrator acts (as does a judge) only on evidence and arguments submitted to him, but he is able to draw the parties' attention to matters of which they may not be aware. He is also able to take the initiative in ascertaining facts and the law. His award must lie between the extremes contended for by the parties. He is, however, expected to use his expertise in assessing the relevance and quality of the evidence and arguments submitted to him.	a. The independent expert has the duty of investigation to discover the facts, details of relevant comparable transactions and all other information relevant to his valuation (though he may receive information regarding these matters from the parties).
b. The arbitrator cannot decide without receiving evidence from the parties, or from one of the parties when he is 'proceeding in default' by the other, except where proceeding on his own initiative.	b. The independent expert bases his decision upon his own knowledge and investigations, but he may be required by the instrument under which he is appointed to receive submissions from the parties.
c. The procedure for arbitration is regulated by the Act.	c. There is no legislation governing procedure for the independent expert and he must therefore settle his own contract with the parties.

d. A party to an arbitration can seek and (through the courts) compel disclosure of documents or the attendance of witnesses.	d. The independent expert has no such powers.
e. An arbitrator may not delegate any of his duties, powers or responsibilities, although he can seek assistance.	e. The independent expert has a duty to use his own knowledge and experience in arriving at his own decision. However, during the course of his investigation the independent expert may seek routine administrative or other assistance from any other person. This is always provided that he is in a position to vouch for the accuracy with which such tasks are carried out.
f. In an arbitration the arbitrator can award that one party shall pay all or part of the arbitrator's fees and all or part of the other party's costs. He can also assess the quantification of those fees and costs.	f. An independent expert has no power to make any orders as to his fees, or as to the costs of a party, unless such a power is conferred upon him by the lease or by agreement between the parties.
g. The arbitrator's fees can be determined by the court under the Act.	g. There is no procedure for formal determination of an independent expert's fees.
h. There is some (albeit limited) right of appeal against the award of an arbitrator on a point of law. An arbitrator's award may also be challenged in the courts on the basis that the arbitrator did not have jurisdiction or on the grounds of 'serious irregularity'. If a serious irregularity is shown the court may (in whole or in part) remit the award, set it aside or declare it to be of no effect.	h. There is no right of appeal against the determination of an expert, though in some circumstances the court might set it aside.
i. Providing he has not acted in bad faith the arbitrator is not liable for negligence.	i. The independent expert is liable in damages for any losses sustained by a party through his negligence. This is so notwithstanding that the court will not interfere with a final and binding determination that he has made.

6.3.1 Expert determination

As appears from the above comparison an expert's functions are different from those of an arbitrator, as is also illustrated by the following case.

Palacath Ltd v Flanagan (1985)

It was held that a surveyor appointed as an expert to determine a rent review is not obliged to make any finding or findings accepting or rejecting the opposing contentions of the parties. Nor is he obliged to accept as valid and binding on him matters on which the parties are agreed. He is not appointed to adjudicate on the cases put forward on behalf of the landlord and tenant but to give his own independent judgment as an expert after reading the representations and valuations of the parties (if any) and giving them such weight as he thinks proper (if any).

6.3.2 Arbitration

An arbitration will normally be governed by the provisions of the *Arbitration Act* 1996 (the '1996 Act'). An arbitration is carried out on the basis of evidence and submissions from each party which the arbitrator then adjudicates upon. The evidence may take the form of written representations with counter-representations or there may be an oral hearing with witnesses attending to explain their valuations and being cross-examined by the other side.

6.4 PROCEDURE IN AN ARBITRATION

Section 34 of the 1996 Act gives the arbitrator a wide range of powers to decide all procedural and evidential matters, subject to the right of the parties to agree any matter. In particular section 34(2) gives the arbitrator power to decide:

(a) when and where any part of the proceedings is to be held;
(b) the language or languages to be used in the proceedings;
(c) whether any, and if so what, form of written statements of

claim and defence are to be used, when these should be supplied and the extent to which such statements can be later amended;

(d) whether any, and if so which, documents or classes of documents should be disclosed between and produced by the parties and at what stage;
(e) whether any, and if so what, questions should be put to and answered by the respective parties and when and in what form this should be done;
(f) whether to apply strict rules of evidence (or any other rules) as to the admissibility, relevance or weight of any material (oral, written or other) sought to be tendered on any matters of fact or opinion, and the time, manner and form in which such material should be exchanged and presented;
(g) whether, and to what extent, the tribunal should itself take the initiative in ascertaining the facts and the law;
(h) whether, and to what extent, there should be oral or written evidence or submissions.

6.4.1 Sanctions for failure to comply with arbitration procedure

By section 34(3) of the 1996 Act, the arbitrator may fix the time within which any directions are to be complied with. By section 41(3), unless the parties agree otherwise, the arbitrator may dismiss a claim if satisfied that there has been inordinate and inexcusable delay on the part of the claimant in pursuing the claim. By section 34(4), if a party fails to attend or be represented at an oral hearing, the arbitrator may proceed in that party's absence. By section 34(5), if without sufficient cause a party fails to comply with any direction, the arbitrator may make a peremptory order. If the party fails to comply with that peremptory order then by section 34(7) the arbitrator may do any of the following:

(a) direct that the party in default shall not be entitled to rely upon any allegation or material which was the subject matter of the order;
(b) draw such adverse inferences from the act of non-compliance as the circumstances justify;
(c) proceed to an award on the basis of such materials as have been properly provided to it;

(d) make such order as it thinks fit as to the payment of costs of the arbitration incurred in consequence of the non-compliance.

6.4.2 Court control over arbitration

As the parties have agreed to resolve their dispute by a particular process the court only has limited control over arbitrations. Of particular importance to rent reviews are:

(a) an application to the court under section 45 to determine a preliminary point of law;
(b) an appeal to the court on a point of law under section 69; and
(c) an application to the court to challenge the award on the ground of serious irregularity under section 68.

The procedure under (a) is considered below. The procedure under (b) and (c) is considered in chapter 7, *Challenging an arbitration award or expert determination*.

6.4.3 Determination of preliminary point of law in an arbitration

Section 45 provides a procedure for the court to determine any question of law arising in the course of the arbitration which the court is satisfied substantially affects the rights of one or more of the parties. However, an application shall not be considered by the court unless:

(a) it is made with the agreement of all the other parties to the proceedings, or
(b) it is made with the permission of the tribunal and the court is satisfied
  (i) that the determination of the question is likely to produce substantial savings in costs, and
  (ii) that the application was made without delay.

First Leisure Trading Ltd v Dorita Properties Ltd (1991)

In this case preliminary issues of law were determined by the Court under the corresponding procedure in the *Arbitration*

Act 1979. The questions concerned whether the arbitrator could find that the actual tenant was a possible hypothetical tenant. It was held that the arbitrator was entitled to find as a fact that the actual tenant would be a potential tenant. Whether or not the actual tenant would be a potential tenant would depend upon the evidence before the arbitrator and his assessment of that evidence.

6.4.4 Evidence in an arbitration

In the case of a determination by an expert it will be for the expert to decide what information or material he wishes to obtain and rely upon in making his determination. In contrast in an arbitration there are two important considerations. They are, first, whether evidence is admissible and, secondly, what weight should be attached to it. If evidence is admissible then it is a matter for the arbitrator as to what weight he can attach to it. If evidence is inadmissible then it should not be placed before the arbitrator. If inadmissible material is placed before the arbitrator and he relies upon it his award may be liable to challenge.

6.4.4.1 Admissibility of evidence: proof of comparables

If the strict rules of evidence are applied comparables will have to be proved strictly.

English Exporters (London) Ltd v Eldonwall Ltd (1973)

In a lease renewal under Part II of the *Landlord and Tenant Act* 1954, it was held that a valuer witness was not entitled to state as fact details of comparables of which he had no direct knowledge. The witness could only rely upon comparables of which he had first hand knowledge or which would be proved by admissible evidence or which were agreed between the parties to the hearing.

Town Centre Securities Ltd v William Morrison Supermarkets Ltd (1982)

The approach in *English Exporters* was applied to a rent review arbitration where an expert gave oral evidence of comparables which were not within his own direct knowledge. However, no objection was taken when the evidence was given with the result that it was held there was an implied waiver of the strict rules of evidence.

English Exporters is an example of the application of the strict rules of evidence which, under section 34(2)(f) of the *Arbitration Act* 1996 (see 6.4), the parties may now agree need not be applied.

6.4.4.2 Admissibility of evidence: post review date comparables and events

Post review date comparables are generally admissible whereas post review date events will not normally be admissible.

Segama NV v Penny Le Roy Ltd (1984)

An arbitrator took into account post-review date comparables in determining the reviewed rent of a shop. It was held that the arbitrator was right to hold that evidence as to rents agreed after the relevant date was admissible. The Court considered that if the rent of comparable premises had been agreed on the day after the relevant date, such an agreement would be of relevance to what the market rent was at the relevant date itself. If the lapse of time before the agreement for comparable premises becomes greater then the evidence will become progressively unreliable as evidence of rental values at the relevant date. The same is no doubt true of rents agreed some time before the relevant date but nobody could suggest that those should be excluded. Hence it was right in principle to admit post review date comparables.

6.4.4.3 **Admissibility of evidence: arbitrators' awards**

Sometimes in a rent review arbitration the parties will seek to rely upon an arbitrator's award or an expert determination as evidence of rental value. If the strict rules of evidence are applied this award or determination is inadmissible.

Land Securities plc v Westminster City Council (1992)

In a rent review arbitration to determine the rental value of a large office block the landlord sought to rely upon an award of an arbitrator in a rent review of a comparable office building. It was held that an arbitrator's award determining the rent of a comparable building was not admissible in another arbitration. The award was held not to be direct evidence of what was happening in the market but an arbitrator's opinion of what would have happened and as such was inadmissible. It was also held that the award was inadmissible as hearsay and that admission of it as evidence might involve an impermissible collateral attack upon the award.

This is another example of the application of the strict rules of evidence which, under section 34(2)(f) the *Arbitration Act* 1996, the parties may agree need not be applied. The objection on the grounds of hearsay has now been overcome by the *Civil Evidence Act* 1995 which allows for the admission of hearsay subject to certain procedural safeguards.

6.4.4.4 **Admissibility of evidence: trading accounts**

In some rent reviews it may be necessary to carry out a profits valuation. This may happen in the case of, for example, leases of hotels, casinos, cinemas, golf courses, petrol filling stations and other unusual properties where the earning capacity of the property is relevant to assessing rental value. In such reviews one party may wish to rely upon the trading accounts of the actual tenant in support of the profits valuation.

Barton (WJ) Ltd v Long Acre Securities Ltd (1982)

In a lease renewal of a baker's shop the County Court judge

ordered discovery of 'all documents relating to trading' at the shop. There were adequate comparables to carry out a valuation in the ordinary way. The Court of Appeal held that the judge was wrong to order discovery as there was no peculiarity in the premises or the business carried on there which would lead to the conclusion that the trading records would be of any assistance. The best evidence of open market rent was what traders in the area were prepared to pay for premises of this type.

Cornwall Coast Country Club Ltd v Cardgrange Ltd (1987)

In a rent review under a lease of a casino the arbitrator refused to order specific discovery relating to the profits earned by the actual tenant. The Court upheld this refusal on the ground that the trading records were not admissible unless they would have been available to prospective tenants in the hypothetical market and these particular records would not have been so available as they were confidential.

6.4.5 Disclosure of documents

By section 34(2)(d) of the 1996 Act, an arbitrator may order disclosure of documents by the parties to the arbitration. By section 43(1), parties to the arbitration may use the same court procedures (i.e. issuing a witness summons) as are available in relation to legal proceedings to secure the attendance of witnesses or the production of documents from a third party. In both cases the witness or the third party may apply to set aside the witness summons.

London & Leeds Estates Ltd v Paribas Ltd (No. 2) (1995)

Witness summonses for the production of documents were issued in a rent review arbitration against the expert in other arbitrations (who was also an expert in the current arbitration) and against an arbitrator in a previous arbitration for previous proofs of evidence. Two of the summonses were set aside by the Court as the information about the documents was 'cryptic in the extreme' and obtained in breach of confidence.

South Tyneside Council v Wickes Building Supplies Ltd (2004)

A witness summons was issued requiring B & Q plc to disclose documents relating to a proposed letting of a unit. The documents were required for use in an arbitration relating to another DIY unit where Wickes was a party as tenant. Wickes and B & Q were competitors in the DIY market. Also, Wickes and B & Q were rival bidders for the proposed letting. The proposed letting contained a confidentiality agreement. B & Q successfully applied to the Court to set aside the witness summons. The judge held that the requirements of confidentiality and respect for B & Q's commercially sensitive information (particularly in the case of a rival such as Wickes) far outweighed any need for disclosure in the arbitration.

6.5 EXPERT EVIDENCE

6.5.1 Duties and responsibilities

Much of the evidence in a rent review will be expert evidence from a valuer. Such an expert is subject to various duties and responsibilities in giving evidence which were summarised in the *Ikarian Reefer*. When giving evidence in court the expert witness will have to comply with the requirements of Part 35 of the *Civil Procedure Rules* 1998. Expert witnesses who are chartered surveyors will also have to comply with the requirements of the RICS for expert witnesses. Each of those is considered below.

National Justice Compania Navieria SA v Prudential Assurance Company Ltd (The Ikarian Reefer) (1993)

In this case the Court summarised the duties of an expert witness as follows.

(a) Expert evidence should be, and should be seen to be, the independent product of the expert uninfluenced as to form or content by the exigencies of litigation.
(b) An expert witness should provide independent assistance by way of objective unbiased opinion in relation to matters within his expertise. An expert witness should not assume the role of an advocate.

(c) An expert witness should state the facts or assumptions upon which his opinion is based. He should not omit to consider material facts which could detract from his concluded opinion.
(d) An expert witness should make it clear when a particular question or issue falls outside his expertise.
(e) If an expert's opinion is not properly researched because he considers that insufficient data is available, then this must be stated with an indication that the opinion is no more than a provisional one. Where an expert witness who has prepared a report could not assert that the report contained the truth, the whole truth and nothing but the truth without some qualification, that qualification should be stated in the report.
(f) If, after exchange of reports, an expert witness changes his view on a material matter having read the other side's expert's report or for any other reason, such change of view should be communicated (through legal representatives) to the other side without delay and when appropriate to the court.
(g) Where expert evidence refers to photographs, plans, calculations, analyses, measurements, survey reports or other similar documents, these must be provided to the opposite party at the same time as the exchange of reports.

6.5.2 RICS practice statement and guidance note: Surveyors Acting as Expert Witnesses

This practice statement applies where any chartered surveyor provides evidence (whether oral or in writing) which may be relied upon by any judicial or quasi-judicial body in the United Kingdom. It applies to evidence given to arbitrators and independent experts. The principal message is that expert evidence provided by a chartered surveyor must be, and must be seen to be, the independent product of the surveyor. The surveyor must also believe that the facts upon which he or she relies are complete and true, and that his or her opinions are correct.

6.5.3 *Civil Procedure Rules*, Part 35

Both the *Civil Procedure Rules* (CPR) Part 35 and the practice direction supplementing it stress the overriding duty of an expert to help the court in matters within his expertise, which duty overrides any obligation to the person from whom he has received instructions or by whom he is paid (CPR 35.3). Part 1 of the practice direction reinforces this duty with the following general requirements:

'(1.2) Expert evidence should be the independent product of the expert uninfluenced by the pressures of litigation.

(1.3) An expert should assist the court by providing objective, unbiased opinion on matters within his expertise, and should not assume the role of an advocate.

(1.4) An expert should consider all material facts, including those which might detract from his opinion.

(1.5) An expert should make it clear:

- (a) when a question or issue falls outside his expertise; and
- (b) when he is not able to reach a definite opinion, for example, because he has insufficient information.

(1.6) If, after producing a report, an expert changes his view on any material matter, such change of view should be communicated to all the parties without delay, and when appropriate to the court.'

6.6 AWARDS, DETERMINATIONS AND COSTS

6.6.1 The arbitration award

In the case of an arbitration award under section 52(1) of the 1996 Act the parties are free to agree on the form of the award. In the absence of agreement (section 52(2) to (5)) the award must:

- be in writing signed by the arbitrator;
- contain the reasons for the award; and
- state the seat of the arbitration and the date when it is made.

In addition, the award should comply with any requirements as to its form in the lease. An award may be interim or final. Where questions of costs are left over for later argument it is normal for the arbitrator to make an interim award, final on all matters except costs.

6.6.2 The expert determination

In the case of a determination by an expert the determination should comply with any requirements as to form in the lease. In addition, good practice requires that it should be in writing, should identify the parties, the lease and the premises and should specify the determination. Normally an expert is under no duty to give reasons.

6.6.3 Costs in an arbitration

In the case of an arbitration, section 61(1) of the 1996 Act provides that the arbitrator may make an award allocating the costs of the arbitration between the parties, subject to any agreement of the parties. By section 61(2), unless the parties agree otherwise, the arbitrator must award costs on the general principle that costs should follow the event, except where it appears to the arbitrator that in the circumstances this is not appropriate in relation to the whole or part of the costs. 'Costs should follow the event' means that the unsuccessful party will be ordered to pay the cost of the successful party.

Parties may seek to protect their positions in costs by making *Calderbank* offers, i.e. an offer which is made without prejudice save as to costs. The offer may then be referred to on the question of costs when the other issues have been resolved – *Calderbank v Calderbank* (1975). It is for this, and other reasons, that an award determining the rent should be final on all matters except costs – so that the parties can consider the award and then make submissions on costs.

6.6.4 Costs in an expert determination

In the case of determination by an expert, he has no power to award costs (including his own fees) unless it is expressly conferred on him by the rent review clause. Thus, in the absence of some express provision, the parties will have to bear their own costs and the expert's fees equally.

7 Challenging an arbitration award or expert determination

7.1 INTRODUCTION

If one of the parties to a contested rent review is dissatisfied with the third party's decision, the dissatisfied party's rights to challenge the decision are limited. The rent review clause itself will not give any right of appeal or review. The dissatisfied party will be left with very limited rights of recourse to the court.

In the case of an arbitration award the rights are contained in sections 68–71 of the *Arbitration Act* 1996 (the '1996 Act') and are, essentially, a challenge on the ground of serious irregularity or an appeal on a point of law.

In the case of an expert determination the rights of recourse are even more limited and are, essentially, either to try to get the determination set aside by the court or to sue the surveyor for negligence.

The reason why the rights of recourse are limited is that the parties have chosen voluntarily to submit their dispute to arbitration or expert determination and so have chosen their own judges and procedures. 'As a consequence it is not unreasonable, although the matter can be more politely expressed, to require them to accept those judges and those procedures "warts and all".' (*King v Thomas McKenna Ltd* (1991) per Lord Donaldson MR)

7.2 CHALLENGING AN ARBITRATION AWARD

7.2.1 Serious irregularity

Section 68 of the 1996 Act provides that a party to arbitral proceedings may (upon notice to the other parties and to the arbitrator) apply to the court challenging the award on the ground of serious irregularity affecting the tribunal, the proceedings or the award. Section 68 provides a procedure under which the court may:

(a) remit the arbitrator's award in whole or in part for consideration;
(b) set the award aside in whole or in part; or
(c) declare the award to be of no effect, in whole or in part.

7.2.2 **Grounds of challenge for serious irregularity**

Section 68(2) provides that serious irregularity means an irregularity of one or more of certain specified grounds which the court considers has caused or will cause substantial injustice to the applicant. The specified grounds (in which the arbitrator is referred to as the tribunal) are:

(a) failure by the tribunal to comply with section 33 (general duty of tribunal);
(b) the tribunal exceeding its powers;
(c) failure by the tribunal to conduct the proceedings in accordance with the procedure agreed by the parties;
(d) failure by the tribunal to deal with all the issues that were put to it;
(e) any arbitral or other institution or person vested by the parties with powers in relation to the proceedings or the award exceeding its powers;
(f) uncertainty or ambiguity as to the effect of the award;
(g) the award being obtained by fraud or the award or the way in which it was procured being contrary to public policy;
(h) failure to comply with the requirements as to the form of the award; or
(i) any irregularity in the conduct of the proceedings or in the award which is admitted by the tribunal or by any arbitral or other institution or person vested by the parties with powers in relation to the proceedings or the award.

7.2.3 **Previous cases on misconduct**

Before looking at cases on serious irregularity it is instructive to look at cases under the corresponding procedure in the

Arbitration Act 1950 (the '1950 Act'). Section 23 of that Act allowed for the removal of the arbitrator or the setting aside of his award in the case of 'misconduct'. This expression was used in a technical rather than a pejorative sense. Most, if not all, of the old cases on misconduct would probably constitute serious irregularity under section 68(2) and are therefore still relevant.

Fox v PG Wellfair Ltd (1981)

In a building arbitration the claimant flat owners were represented but the builders and the NHBC were not. The arbitrator rejected a large amount of the claimant's expert evidence and awarded only a fraction of the claim. His award was set aside on the ground of misconduct. Lord Denning MR described the arbitrator's duties as follows.

> 'His [the arbitrator's] function is not to supply evidence of the defendants but to adjudicate upon the evidence given before him. He can and should use his special knowledge so as to understand the evidence that is given in the letters that have passed, the usage of the trade, the dealings in the market and to appreciate the worth of all that he sees upon a view. But he cannot use his special knowledge or at any rate he should not use it so as to provide evidence on behalf of the defendants which they have not chosen to provide for themselves. For then he would be discarding the role of an impartial arbitrator and assuming the role of advocate for the defaulting side. At any rate he should not use his own knowledge to derogate from the evidence of the plaintiffs' experts without putting his own knowledge to them and giving them a chance of answering it and showing that his view is wrong.'

Whilst this was a building contract case, the statements of principle are equally applicable to rent review arbitrations.

Zermalt Holdings SA v No-Life Upholstery Repairs Ltd (1985)

A rent review of a shop was dealt with by exchange of written submissions. The landlord challenged the award under section 23 of the 1950 Act alleging that the arbitrator had based his decision in part on two matters (a description of the premises as a developers' shell and not analysing by extrapolating from much smaller comparables) never previously referred to by either party or by the arbitrator and which appeared for the first time in his award. It was held that the arbitrator had relied upon 'an unavoidable inclination' to rely upon his own expertise. It was 'not right that a decision should be based on specific matters which the parties have never had the chance to deal with, nor is it right that a party should first learn of adverse points in the decision against him'. The award was set aside and the arbitrator was removed.

Top Shop Estates Ltd v C Danino (1985)

An arbitrator's award was challenged under section 23 of the 1950 Act on the grounds that he had 'taken account of his own knowledge' by inspecting the comparables without indicating in his directions that he intended to do so and had failed to alert the parties or allow them the opportunity to comment in relation to it. Also the arbitrator had conducted a 'series of pedestrian counts' and had again failed to draw this to the attention of the parties. The arbitrator also 'validated' inadmissible evidence from the respondents' surveyor, failing both to disclose the evidence and allow comments from the applicants. It was held that the arbitrator had acted under a misapprehension of his function as an arbitrator. He had used his expert knowledge in the case to aid his understanding, but he had also 'supplied' it in the form of evidence, which was not requested by the parties. Although there was no 'imputation upon the personal conduct' of the arbitrator, the award was set aside and an order for the arbitrator's removal was made.

Techno Ltd v Allied Dunbar Assurance plc (1993)

In a rent review arbitration the parties prepared an agreed statement of facts which included the agreed assumption that the property to be valued was of a certain height, construction and layout. In his award the arbitrator ignored the agreed assumption and concluded that the tenant's surveyor had misdirected himself in applying to his analysis part of the agreed assumption. He made an award on a basis which omitted part of the agreed assumption. It was held that the arbitrator had failed in his obligations and accordingly the interim award was remitted to the arbitrator. The arbitrator was not entitled to disregard the assumption contained in the statement of facts. In addition, the statement of facts was held to constitute a binding contract, although one of 'special character'. The arbitrator retained a discretion not to apply the agreed terms and conditions, but an opportunity for both parties to comment and be heard should have been proffered before the arbitrator departed from it.

Handley v Nationwide Anglia Building Society (1992)

The applicant sought to set aside a rent review award upon the following four grounds:

(1) that there was no evidence to justify certain reductions made by the arbitrator;
(2) that a further reduction was made incorrectly in respect of a planning restriction;
(3) that the arbitrator excluded a transaction in relation to a property even though evidence to the contrary was available; and
(4) that the arbitrator had made a further reduction based upon his own expert view that the property was in a less favourable trading area than other comparable properties.

The court held that the award should be set aside on the first and fourth grounds. There had been a failure to give the parties adequate 'opportunity to comment on the figures which the arbitrator pulled out of his own experience and his own perception'.

Henry Sotheran Ltd v Norwich Union Life Insurance Society (1992)

The court considered the failure of an arbitrator to hold an oral hearing when requested by one party to do so. There was an agreement between the parties that the arbitration would be held via written representations. However the right to request an oral hearing was reserved. At a later date, the tenant's surveyor expressed doubts as to the information provided by the landlord's expert and the applicants requested an oral hearing which the arbitrator acceded to. However, following a lengthy period of correspondence between all the parties, the arbitrator informed them that he had made his award. It was held that the arbitrator has a duty to offer a party an oral hearing if the party legitimately believes he is entitled to one. The arbitrator had failed in his duty to act judicially and to receive submissions from both parties, whether he considers that the submissions are really going to assist him or not. The case was remitted to a new arbitrator for a hearing.

Mount Charlotte Investments plc v Prudential Assurance Company Ltd (1995)

In a rent review of a hotel conducted on written representations the arbitrator directed that certain transactions were inadmissible and that he would make an unaccompanied inspection of the subject premises. In his award he considered written representations from the landlord's surveyor containing inadmissible details of comparables and stated that he had inspected other hotels in the area. It was held that the arbitrator had failed to pay heed to his own directions, that misconduct had occurred and that the award should be set aside and remitted to another arbitrator.

All these cases were decided under section 23 of the 1950 Act which required proof of 'misconduct'. The test now under the 1996 Act is whether there has been a serious irregularity which the court considers has caused or will cause substantial injustice.

7.2.4 Cases on serious irregularity under the 1996 Act

In order to succeed in a challenge under section 68 of the 1996 Act, the applicant must show that there has been an irregularity within one or more of the specified grounds which the court considers has caused or will cause substantial injustice to the applicant.

Egmetra AG v Marco Trading Corpn (1999)

In this case the Court said that:

> 'The test of "substantial injustice" is intended to be applied by way of support of the arbitral process, not by way of interference with that process. Thus it is only in those cases where it can be said that what has happened is so far removed from what could reasonably be expected of the arbitral process that we would expect the Court to take action ... In short, section 68 is really designed as a long stop, only available in extreme cases where the tribunal has gone so wrong in its conduct of the arbitration that justice calls out for it to be corrected'
>
> and that
>
> '[section 68] is no soft option clause as an alternative to a failed application for leave to appeal'.

Checkpoint Ltd v Strathclyde Pension Fund (2003)

An arbitrator was appointed to determine the rent for storage and distribution premises in Bracknell. The landlord's surveyor relied upon transactions in a location about six miles away. The tenant's surveyor rejected those transactions as not being comparable and relied upon a comparable in Bracknell and evidence of oversupply and poor demand in the immediate locality of the subject premises. In his award the arbitrator referred to his personal knowledge and experience of transactions in the area of the six transactions, rejected the tenant's comparable and failed to address the tenant's evidence concerning oversupply and poor demand. The arbitrator accepted the landlord's valuation. The Court of Appeal held that there was no serious irregularity. It was not unfair for the arbitrator to use knowledge in the form of information of the kind, and within the range, of knowledge one would reasonably expect the arbitrator to have acquired if, as required by the lease, he was experienced in the letting and/or valuation of property of a similar nature to the subject premises. As the question of oversupply had only a subordinate evidential character it did not need to be resolved under section 68(2)(d).

Warborough Investments Ltd v S Robinson and Sons (Holdings) Ltd (2003)

An arbitrator determined the reviewed rent for a light industrial estate in Derby. The arbitrator relied upon comparables before him and made a 41% adjustment to reflect a complete prohibition on retail use. The landlord alleged that there was a serious irregularity in that there was no evidence to support the 41% deduction.

It was held that sufficient matters had been put into the arena which allowed the arbitrator to act as he did and that, if there had been an irregularity, the case that the landlord's surveyor might have put, had he had an opportunity of addressing the arbitrator's approach, would not have been so different as to justify the conclusion that the lack of that opportunity itself caused a substantial injustice.

Guardcliffe Properties Ltd v City and St James (2003)

An arbitrator determined the reviewed rent for commercial premises in Newcastle-upon-Tyne at £35,000 which included a downward adjustment of £10,000 to reflect a hypothetical rent-free period and a deduction of £5,500 to reflect the tenant's ongoing liabilities both of which issues had not been raised by either party. He also assumed that in a comparable involving the payment of a premium, the whole of it was attributable to fit-out costs when only a small part was so attributable.

The Court held that the award should be remitted to the arbitrator as the making of the two deductions would cause substantial injustice to the landlord whose surveyor had been denied the chance to refute the appropriateness of the deductions. As there was no factual basis for the treatment of the premium that also was a serious irregularity.

St George's Investment Co v Gemini Consulting Ltd (2004)

A rent review arbitration was conducted by way of written representations in relation to lower-ground-floor business premises in Knightsbridge. The tenants also occupied the third floor of the property under a separate tenancy, for which a revised rent had already been set.

Both parties agreed that external comparables were of little assistance and that the appropriate valuation method was to take the reviewed rent for the third floor and apply a discount. The focus of their dispute was upon the calculation of this discount. The tenants' expert also submitted an alternative method based upon the external comparables. Under this method, he applied a discount to the comparables because the lease contained more onerous terms.

The arbitrator accepted the third-floor discount method and applied a discount of 40% from the third-floor rent. He then applied an additional discount for the onerous terms in the lease.

The landlords applied to remit the award owing to this additional discount. Their application was allowed by a deputy judge of the Chancery Division. He observed that although the tenants' valuer had mentioned a discount for onerous terms, he had done so only in relation to the external comparables. In relation to the third-floor discount approach, neither party had suggested any discount for onerous terms. Accordingly, the question of whether the third-floor adjusted rent should be subjected to a discount for the onerous terms had not been 'put into the arena' before the arbitrator. It followed that there had been a serious irregularity.

This irregularity had caused substantial injustice to the landlords. Had the landlords been given the opportunity to address the arbitrator on the issue, he would have realised that the third-floor rent had itself been adjusted to reflect the onerous terms and he would therefore have rejected a further discount. Accordingly, it was right to remit the award to the arbitrator.

7.2.5 Appeal on a point of law under section 69

Unless otherwise agreed by the parties, a party to an arbitration may (upon notice to the other parties and to the arbitrator) appeal to the court on a question of law arising out of an award (section 69 of the 1996 Act). However, an appeal shall not be brought except either (a) with the agreement of all other parties or (b) with the leave of the court (section 69(2)). Under section 69(3), the court will only give leave if it is satisfied:

'(a) that the determination of the question will substantially affect the rights of one or more of the parties,

(b) that the question is one which the tribunal was asked to determine,

(c) that, on the basis of the findings of fact in the award:

  (i) the decision of the tribunal on the question is obviously wrong, or

  (ii) the question is one of general public importance and the decision of the tribunal is at least open to serious doubt, and

(d) that, despite the agreement of the parties to resolve the matter by arbitration, it is just and proper in all the circumstances for the court to determine the question.'

It can be seen that there are formidable obstacles facing a party wishing to appeal against a rent review award on a point of law. The difficulties are well illustrated by the following cases where leave to appeal was refused.

Marklands Ltd v Virgin Retail Ltd (2004)

In an application for leave to appeal it was argued that the arbitrator had erred in law in his treatment of the hypothetical negotiations between the willing lessor and the willing lessee. In particular, it was said that the willing lessor could as part of those negotiations threaten to deal with the property in the fashion which he thought most appropriate and advantageous to him unless the tenant was willing to pay a sufficiently high and acceptable rent in order to secure the hypothetical lease. It was held that leave should not be granted because section 69(1) only deals with 'a question of law arising out of an award' and as the arbitrator had not dealt with the alleged point there could be no question of law arising out of the award.

BLCT (13096) Ltd v J Sainsbury plc (2003)

In a rent review of a food superstore in Cambridge the arbitrator had to consider a comparable comprising a new ASDA store a mile away where a rent of £18 per sq ft plus a premium of £3m had been paid. The parties' valuers did not agree how to analyse the comparable and in particular whether the premium should be decapitalised and treated as part of the rent. The arbitrator preferred the tenant's approach which ignored the premium and held that it was a key money payment with no evidence that it could be treated as a payment in lieu of rent. The landlord sought leave to appeal which was refused on various grounds including that it was not clear what were the suggested questions of law.

In contrast to the above cases where leave to appeal was refused, where there is a question of law arising out of the award which the arbitrator was asked to decide, then leave may be granted if the decision of the arbitrator is either obviously wrong or the question is one of general public importance and the decision of the arbitrator is at least open to serious doubt. In the field of rent review, it is difficult to see how a question might be of general public importance unless the point impacts on many other rent reviews or concerns a term in widespread use in a common form of lease. This means that in most rent review cases at the stage of the application for leave the question will be whether the decision is obviously wrong.

Bisichi Mining Ltd v Bass Holdings Ltd (2002)

The rent under a sublease was reviewable in certain years 'of the said term'. The question arose whether this meant from the date of grant or the date from which the term was expressed to run. The arbitrator decided that it meant the latter. Leave to appeal was granted on the basis that this was obviously wrong and the appeal was allowed on the grounds that the 'said term' meant the term granted from the date of the sublease.

Durley House Ltd v Cadogan (2000)

A rent review clause provided for the disregard of improvements and incorporated section 34 of the *Landlord and Tenant Act* 1954 by reference. Improvements were carried out by a third party under an agreement with the tenant. The arbitrator decided that these improvements were not to be disregarded because they were not carried out by the tenant. Leave to appeal was granted on the basis that this was obviously wrong. On the appeal it was held that given the statutory language of section 34 a tenant will normally satisfy the statutory requirement if he can establish that he physically effected the works himself or got a third party to do so. In this case the extent of the involvement of the tenant was quite sufficient to say that it 'carried out' the improvements with the result that the arbitrator had erred in law and the appeal was allowed.

7.2.6 Procedure under sections 68 and 69

By section 70(3) of the 1996 Act, any application or appeal must be brought within 28 days of the date of the award. The expression 'the date of the award' is defined in section 54(2) as the date upon which the arbitrator signed the award. This means that the time for an application or appeal may start running before the parties have the award. It is therefore important for the parties to take up the award promptly otherwise the time for challenge may expire before the parties know what the award says. There is provision in section 80(5) for the 28-day time limit to be extended but the courts are likely to exercise this power sparingly with the result that applications made out of time may well fail. Under both procedures (i.e. section 68 and 69) notice of the proceedings must be given to the arbitrator. Applications for leave to appeal against an arbitrator's award are normally dealt with on paper and without a hearing (section 69(5)). It is not a breach of the parties' human rights for the application to be dealt with on paper: *BLCT (13096) Ltd v J Sainsbury plc* (2003).

By section 73, a party may lose the right to object under section 68. If a party takes part, or continues to take part, in the proceedings without making any objection that the proceedings have been improperly conducted or that there has been a failure to comply with the arbitration agreement or with any provision of the Act or that there has been any other irregularity affecting the tribunal or the proceedings, then he may not raise that objection later unless he did not know and could not with reasonable diligence have discovered the grounds for the objection.

7.2.7 Further appeal

In the case of a serious irregularity application under section 68, an appeal to the Court of Appeal may only be made with the leave of 'the court'. This expression means the judge deciding the application. If that judge refuses leave to appeal that is an end to the matter. In the case of an application for leave to appeal under section 69, by section 69(6), the leave of 'the court' is required for any appeal from a decision of the court to grant or refuse leave to appeal. This expression means the court of first instance: *Henry Boot Construction (UK) v Malmaison Hotel (Manchester) Ltd* (2000). The same applies to any decision of the court in an actual appeal under section 69. However, the court should not give leave to appeal to the Court of Appeal unless it considers the question is one of general importance or is one which for some other special reason should be considered by the Court of Appeal (section 69(8)).

Henry Boot Construction (UK) Ltd v Malmaison Hotel (Manchester) Ltd (2000)

The applicants sought leave to appeal to the Court of Appeal from the previous decision of a judge to dismiss their appeal against an arbitrator's interim award under section 69(1) of the *Arbitration Act* 1996. In the alternative, they sought a review of the judge's decision to refuse leave to appeal under section 69(8) of the same Act.

It was held that the Court of Appeal had no jurisdiction either to grant leave or to review that refusal to grant leave. Upon a proper construction of section 69(8) of the 1996 Act, leave to appeal may only be granted by the High Court or the County Court in such circumstances. It was also held that section 55 of the *Access to Justice Act* 1999 (the '1999 Act') did not affect section 69(8) as it would appear contrary to the philosophy of the 1999 Act generally to permit two applications for permission to appeal.

7.3 CHALLENGING AN EXPERT DETERMINATION

In the case of an expert determination there are essentially three possible remedies. Firstly, if there is fraud or collusion the determination could be set aside. Secondly, in very limited circumstances the determination may be set aside if carried out on a wholly erroneous basis. Thirdly, if the expert is negligent it may be possible to sue him for damages for professional negligence. However the expert's liability in negligence does not affect the determination which remains binding between the parties.

7.3.1 Fraud or collusion

If there is fraud or collusion with the other party then the award could be set aside. There is no reported case concerning fraud or collusion in a rent review determination. However, the basic principle is that fraud unravels all. This principle is well illustrated by the following landlord and tenant case.

Rous v Mitchell (1991)

A notice to quit an agricultural holding alleged breaches of covenant comprising the subletting of cottages. In fact, the landlord had consented to or acquiesced in the sublettings and the notice was therefore held to be dishonest and a nullity on the grounds that fraud unravels all.

7.3.2 Wholly erroneous basis

The court may set aside an expert determination in two situations because it is made on a wholly erroneous basis. The first is where there is a manifest error in the determination. In other words there must be an error on the face of the award. Such cases are rare in rent reviews. The second is where there is a material departure by the expert from his instructions. In this category, it does not matter if the expert answers the right question in the wrong way. In that situation the determination will still be binding. In this category, what is necessary is that the expert answers the wrong question. The fact of the matter is that the parties have entrusted the decision to the expert and it is not for the court to substitute its own opinion.

Jones v Sherwood Computer Services plc (1992)

In this case the Court of Appeal described this approach as follows:

> 'If the parties to an agreement have referred a matter which is within the expertise of the accountancy profession to accountants to determine, and have agreed that the determination is to be conclusive, final and binding for all purposes, and the chosen accountants have made their determination, it does not seem appropriate that the Court should rush in to substitute its own opinion, with the assistance of further accountants' evidence, for the determination of the chosen accountants'.

This was a share valuation case in which the claimants contended that the advice provided by an accountancy firm, acting in their capacity as experts, failed to consider material which was vital to a contract between them and the defendants.

It was held on appeal that where parties agreed to be bound by an expert's award it may not be challenged in the courts if the expert has followed the instructions given by the parties. In order to ascertain whether an expert had acted correctly the first step must be to see what task the parties had remitted to the expert. The nature of any mistake must then be considered, for any mistake resulting from a departure from the instructions may be considered a breach of the expert's obligations if the expert has not done what he was appointed to do.

The relevant principles were further considered by the Court of Appeal in *Norwich Union Life Insurance Society v P&O Property Holdings Ltd* (1993) and the House of Lords in *Mercury Communications Ltd v Director General of Telecommunications* (1996).

British Shipbuilders v VSEL Consortium plc (1997)

In this case the Court summarised the effect of *Jones, Norwich Union* and *Mercury* as follows:

(1) The role of the expert, the ambit of his remit (or jurisdiction) and the character of his remit are a matter of construction of the agreement.

(2) If the agreement confers upon the expert the exclusive remit to determine a question, (subject to (3) and (4) below) the jurisdiction of the court to determine that question is excluded. It is irrelevant whether the court would have reached a different conclusion or considers that the expert's decision is wrong, because the parties agreed to abide by the decision of the expert.

(3) If the expert goes outside his remit, e.g. by determining a different question from that remitted or by failing to comply with any conditions which the agreement requires him to comply with in making his determination, the court may intervene and set his decision aside.

(4) The court may also set aside a decision of the expert where the agreement so provides if his determination discloses a manifest error.

(5) The court has jurisdiction ahead of an expert determination to determine the limits of his remit or the conditions which the expert must comply with, but will usually decline to do so. This is because the question would generally only be relevant if one party considers that the expert got the decision wrong. To apply to the court in anticipation of a decision would be a waste of time and money – the saving of which is presumed to have been relevant to agreeing to the determination by the expert.

JT Sydenham and Co Ltd v Enichem Elastomers Ltd (1989)

The claimant sought to challenge the rent determination made by the expert, who was appointed under the rent review provisions of the lease. The claimant challenged the independent surveyor's interpretation of two tenants' covenants. The independent surveyor's interpretation was set aside, because he had misconstrued the user clause with the result that his determination was a nullity and not binding on the parties.

Apus Properties Ltd v Douglas Farrow and Co Ltd and Others (1989)

The claimants contended that the independent expert instructed under the rent review clause had failed to disregard improvements to the property and misconstrued the user covenant. It was held that the expert's construction of a modification of user condition was sufficient to invalidate the award and the expert had misconstrued the modification. The improvements challenge failed because there was nothing in the determination to show that the expert had wrongly taken improvements into account.

Nikko Hotels (UK) Ltd v MEPC Ltd (1991)

An expert was appointed to determine the rent of a hotel by reference to a formula depending upon 'the average room rate'. An issue arose whether this meant the published tariff or the published tariff with any available discounts. The expert determined the issue in favour of the landlord and the tenant applied for a declaration that the decision was a nullity. The Court declined to set aside the decision as the issue was remitted to the expert by contract and he answered that question which was therefore binding on the parties whether right or wrong.

Pontsarn Investments Ltd v Kansallis-Osake-Pankki (1992)

This was an application by the defendant in the case to strike out a paragraph in the summons issued by the claimant, by which the claimant sought to establish that the expert's determination was void. The claimant contended that the expert had failed in his interpretation and determination of the open market rent for the property. It was held by the Court that the decision of the expert in this instance was binding and not subject to review. It was held that the position of an expert differs from that of other tribunals, for it 'is settled as a matter of contract between the parties. It is not imposed from without'.

Morgan Sindall plc v Sawston Farms (Cambs) Ltd (1999)

The claimant sought to appeal the decision of the judge who had dismissed its claim for declaratory relief that the opinion of an expert surveyor was a nullity on the basis that he had used an incorrect approach in valuing the property and that he had valued the wrong subject matter. It was held that it was a question of what the expert had been required to place a value upon as instructed by the instructing parties. Any mistakes made by the expert in this case were a result of the parties' formulation of the task to be undertaken by the expert. The valuation had been a 'non-speaking' valuation with the expert's reasoning and calculations concealed. It was not for the Court 'to attempt to infer, from ambiguous shadows and murmurs, what is happening behind the curtain'.

7.3.3 Liability of the expert in negligence

The other remedy for a disappointed party in the case of an expert's determination is to sue the expert for negligence. The cases show that it is not easy to establish liability in negligence.

Belvedere Motors Ltd v King (1981)

A rent review clause provided that if the parties were unable to agree a new rent an independent valuer should be appointed and act as an expert. The defendant was appointed and received written submissions from the parties. The landlord's surveyor contended that the new rent should be £20,765. The tenant's surveyor argued for £12,000. The defendant fixed the rent at £15,000. The landlord sued the defendant for professional negligence. It was alleged that his figure was so significantly below the 'right' figure that he was guilty of negligence. Also, the actual method adopted by the valuer in making his valuation was subjected to detailed criticisms. It was held that the expert owed the parties a duty to use the reasonable care and skill of such persons of ordinary competence measured by the professional standard of the time, but that on a consideration of all the evidence the expert had not been negligent in assessing the new rent.

Zubaida v Hargreaves (1993)

In a rent review of restaurant premises the defendant was appointed by the President of the RICS to act as an expert. The claimant contended for a rent of £13,000 per annum. The landlord contended for a rent of £50,000 per annum. The defendant determined the rent to be £27,000 per annum. The claimant sued the defendant for damages for negligence primarily on the ground that the defendant used retail comparables whereas he should have used only restaurant comparables. The judge held that the defendant carried out his duties as an independent expert with competence and without negligence and that the criticisms made of him were unjustified. He said that the relevant principles of law were well established:

- 'An independent expert, unlike an arbitrator, does not have immunity from being sued for negligence. He has duties to both parties and is liable in damages if he causes loss to either of them by failure to take due care or to exercise reasonable professional skill in carrying out his duties.
- He will not be guilty of negligence if he acted in accordance with the practice of competent professional opinion; and where there is a difference of opinion in the profession if he has acted in accordance with the practice accepted as proper by a substantial number of persons in his profession.
- The task of valuation rarely admits of a precise conclusion. Often there are many imponderables. Experts using care may arrive at different conclusions without anyone being justified in saying that any of them did so through incompetence or lack of care.
- It is not the task of the court to seek to replace an independent expert's figure with some other figure determined by it, but to determine only whether the independent expert omitted to consider some matter which he ought to have considered, or took into account matters which he ought not to have taken into account, or in some other way failed to adopt the procedure and practice accepted as standard in his profession.
- If the rent determined by the independent expert in an individual case is significantly outside the bracket which

> the evidence shows to be acceptable, that may be evidence of negligence on his part.'

In addition the judge noted:

> 'Whether an independent surveyor should make enquiries of his own in regard to comparables other than those presented to him must be a matter of judgment in the particular circumstances of the case. Where the parties are professionally represented by surveyors it is unlikely to be necessary. It may be different where one or both are not so represented. However, it must be borne in mind that not all comparables subsequently produced when an independent expert's valuation is challenged might have been discovered by him on an enquiry conducted with reasonable diligence.'

Wallshire Ltd v Aarons (1989)

A lease provided for the rent to be reviewed to the open market rental value which, in default of agreement, was to be determined by an independent surveyor acting as an expert. The premises demised by the lease comprised a ground floor shop with a self-contained maisonette above, which was sublet on a regulated tenancy at an annual rent of £1,508. Having received submissions (which referred to 13 allegedly comparable transactions) from each party, and having investigated (and rejected as unhelpful) another comparable and inspected the premises, the expert determined the rent at £6,600. He discounted by 10% the rent payable for the main comparable to disregard goodwill, as the rent review clause directed, and discounted the maisonette rent to £1,000 to reflect the expense of the inferior landlord's repairing and insuring obligations.

The landlord sued the expert for negligently valuing the premises at a figure which was far too low and inappropriately deducting expenses in valuing the maisonette. The judge held that, although there were further inquiries which the expert could have made regarding the main comparable, such inquiries would have been unlikely to have elicited any useful information. The expert had been right in his treatment of goodwill. Also, a reasonable surveyor was justified in coming to the conclusion that catering rents were of no or very little assistance in calculating the rents of a shop. The expert acted reasonably in taking the view that he had sufficient comparables to make it unnecessary for him to make further inquiries. The expert's approach to the maisonette could not be faulted, as a hypothetical reasonable tenant taking a lease of a shop would view a flat or maisonette above the shop as something of a nuisance.

Currys Group plc v Martin (1999)

Retail premises were demised to the claimant for a term of 25 years at a rent subject to five-yearly reviews. At review on 13 January 1993, the defendant was nominated by the President of the RICS to determine the rent, acting as an independent expert. It became clear that the parties' interpretations of the lease varied and the expert took advice from a legal assessor, which was to the effect that the open market rent was to be determined on the basis of a 'headline rent'. On that basis, the landlord's valuer contended for a market rent of £110,250 (£65 per sq ft). The tenant's valuer contended that there was no justification for any increase in the passing rent of £72,000. It was common ground that the hypothetical landlord must be assumed to be the owner of the shopping centre and not merely of the demised premises. The parties also agreed that three very recent open market transactions in the centre were particularly relevant, two of which (numbers 14 and 17) had involved headline rents of £65 per sq ft. The expert arrived at his determination in April 1994, at which time it was known that the tenants of numbers 14 and 17 had ceased trading and vacated their premises. The expert did not reflect that knowledge in his determination, in which he concluded that the hypothetical landlord would have been willing to offer the hypothetical tenant inducements sufficient to obtain a headline rent reflecting £65 per sq ft. He determined that the revised rent should be £107,000 per annum.

The tenant sued the expert and claimed damages of £800,000. It was held that the expert had not been negligent. It was necessary for the claimant to show that the defendant's determination was one which no reasonably competent surveyor could have reached. The defendant had been correct (or at any rate non-negligent) to disregard evidence of subsequent events.

Lewisham Investment Partnership Ltd v Morgan (1997)

The predecessor in title of the claimant let a unit in the Lewisham Centre to Marks & Spencer plc for a term of 100 years at a rent subject to review. The lease entitled the tenant to underlet not more than three separate parts of the premises. The defendant expert determined the market rent at £250,000 per annum. In reaching this determination, the defendant employed an overall method, rather than a zoning method and consulted an experienced property solicitor who advised him that he was bound by the decision of the Court of Appeal in *Iceland Frozen Foods v Starlight Investments*. The defendant therefore considered that he could not value the hypothetical lease on the basis that the hypothetical tenant would be permitted to underlet the unit in not more than three separate parts.

The claimant sued the defendant for damages for negligence, contending that the market rent was £430,000 per annum, and that the rent determined by the defendant was lower than that which a reasonably competent surveyor in the defendant's position could have determined.

It was held, given the size of the unit, in particular the ratio between its frontage and depth, that the defendant had not been negligent in not applying the zoning method as his principal method of valuation. Also, the defendant had been entitled to rely upon the legal advice he had received, which correctly set out the effect of the decision of the Court of Appeal in the *Iceland* case.

Index

The Case in Point Series

The *Case in Point* series is an exiting new set of concise practical guides to legal issues in land, property and construction. Written for the property professional, they get straight to the key issues in a refreshingly jargon-free style.

Areas covered:

Negligence in Valuation and Surveys
Stock code: 6388
Published: December 2002

Party Walls
Stock code: 7269
Published: May 2004

Service Charges
Stock code: 7272
Published: June 2004

Estate Agency
Stock code: 7472
Published: July 2004

Lease Renewal
Due to publish: Summer 2005

If you would like to be kept informed when new *Case in Point* titles are published, please e-mail rbmarketing@rics.org.uk

How to order:
All RICS Books titles can be ordered direct by:
☎ Telephoning 0870 333 1600 (Option 3)
🖱 Online at www.ricsbooks.com
⌨ E-mail mailorder@rics.org.uk